Contents

J

J CONTENTS

What is an Approved Document?

This document has been approved and issued by the Secretary of State to provide practical guidance on ways of complying with Requirements J1 to J6 and regulations 7 of the Building Regulations 2000 (SI 2000/2531) for England and Wales, as amended. The Building Regulations 2000 are referred to throughout the remainder of this Document as 'the Building Regulations'. Where appropriate the Approved Document also gives guidance on relevant requirements in the Building (Approved Inspectors etc) Regulations 2000 (SI 2000/2532), as amended.

The intention of issuing Approved Documents is to provide guidance about compliance with specific aspects of building regulations in some of the more common building situations. They set out what, in ordinary circumstances, may be reasonable provision for compliance with the relevant requirement(s) of building regulations to which they refer.

If guidance in an Approved Document is followed there will be a presumption of compliance with the requirement(s) covered by the guidance. However, this presumption can be overturned, so simply following guidance does not guarantee compliance. For example, if one particular case is unusual in some way, then 'normal' guidance may not be applicable. It is also important to note that there may well be other ways of achieving compliance with the requirements. **There is therefore no obligation to adopt any particular solution contained in this Approved Document if you would prefer to meet the relevant requirement in some other way. However, persons intending to carry out building work should always check with their Building Control Body, either the local authority or an approved inspector, that their proposals comply with building regulations.**

The guidance contained in this Approved Document relates only to the particular requirements of building regulations that the document addresses (see 'Requirements' below). However, building work may be subject to more than one requirement of building regulations. In such cases the work will also have to comply with any other applicable requirements of building regulations.

This document is one of a series that has been approved and issued by the Secretary of State for the purpose of providing practical guidance with respect to the requirements of Schedule 1 and Regulation 7 of the Building Regulations 2000 (SI 2000/2531) (as amended) for England and Wales.

At the back of this document is a list of all the documents that have been approved and issued by the Secretary of State for this purpose.

How to use this Approved Document

In this document the following conventions have been adopted to assist understanding and interpretation:

a. Text shown against a green background are extracts from the Building Regulations or Building (Approved Inspectors etc) Regulations, both as amended, and set out the legal requirements that relate to compliance with the sanitation, hot water safety and water efficiency requirements of building regulations. It should be remembered however that, as noted above, building works must comply with all the other applicable provisions of building regulations.

b. Key terms are defined in Section 0 and are printed in *italic text*.

c. Details of technical publications referred to in the text of this Document will be given in footnotes and repeated as end notes. A reference to a publication is likely to be made for one of two main reasons. The publication may contain additional or more comprehensive technical detail, which it would be impractical to include in full in the Document but which is needed to fully explain ways of meeting the requirements; or it is a source of more general information. The reason for the reference will be indicated in each case. The reference will be to a specified edition of the document. The Approved Document may be amended from time to time to include new references or to refer to revised editions where this aids compliance.

Where you can get further help

If you do not understand the technical guidance or other information set out in this Approved Document and the additional detailed technical references to which it directs you, there are a number of routes through which you can seek further assistance:

- The Communities and Local Government website: www.communities.gov.uk

- The Planning Portal website: www.planningportal.gov.uk

- If you are the person undertaking the building work you can seek assistance either from your local authority building control service or from your approved inspector (depending on which building control service you are using, or intend to use, to certify compliance of your work with the requirements of the Building Regulations).

- Persons registered with a competent person self-certification scheme may be able to get technical advice from their scheme operator.

- If your query is of a highly technical nature you may wish to seek the advice of a specialist, or industry technical body, for the relevant subject.

Responsibility for compliance

It is important to remember that if you are the person (e.g. designer, builder, installer) carrying out building work to which any requirement of building regulations applies you have a responsibility to ensure that the work complies with any such requirement. The building owner may also have a responsibility for ensuring compliance with building regulation requirements and could be served with an enforcement notice in cases of non-compliance.

The requirements

This Approved Document, which takes effect on 1 October 2010, deals with combustion appliances and fuel storage systems in the Building Regulations 2000 (as amended)

Limitation on requirements

In accordance with regulation 8 of the Building Regulations, the requirements in Parts A to D, F to K and N and P (except for paragraphs G2, H2 and J6) of Schedule 1 to the Building Regulations do not require anything to be done except for the purpose of securing reasonable standards of health and safety for persons in or about buildings (and any others who may be affected by buildings or matters connected with buildings).

Paragraph G2 is excluded from regulation 8 as it deals with the conservation of water. Paragraphs H2 and J6 are excluded from regulation 8 because they deal directly with prevention of the contamination of water and of oil pollution. Parts E and M (which deal, respectively, with resistance to the passage of sound and access to and use of buildings) are excluded from regulation 8 because they address the welfare and convenience of building users. Part L is excluded from regulation 8 because it addresses the conservation of fuel and power. All these matters are amongst the purposes, other than health and safety that may be addressed by Building Regulations.

Types of work covered by this Approved Document

Building work

Building work, as defined in regulation 3 of the Building Regulations 2000, includes the erection and extension of a building, the provision or extension of a controlled service or fitting, and the material alteration of a building or a controlled service or fitting. In addition, Building Regulations may apply in cases where the purposes for which or the manner or circumstances in which a building or part of a building is used change in the way that constitutes a material change of use. Under regulation 4 of the Building Regulations 2000 (as amended), building work should be carried out in such a way that, on completion of work,

i. the building complies with the applicable Parts of Schedule 1 to the Building Regulations,

ii. in the case of an extension or material alteration of a building, or the provision, extension or material alteration of a controlled service or fitting, where it did not comply with any such requirement, it is no more unsatisfactory in relation to that requirement than before the work was carried out.

Work described in Part J concerns the provision or extension of controlled services or fittings. Work associated with installations covered in these sections may be subject to other relevant Parts of the Building Regulations.

Material change of use

A material change of use occurs in specified circumstances in which a building or part of a building that was previously used for one purpose will be used in future for another. Where there is a material change of use the Building Regulations set requirements that must be met before the building can be used for its new purpose.

Regulation 5 of the Building Regulations specifies the following circumstances as material changes of use:

*   a building is used as a dwelling where previously it was not.

*   a building contains a flat where previously it did not.

*   a building is used as an hotel or boarding house where previously it was not.

*   a building is used as an institution where previously it was not.

*   a building is used as a public building where previously it was not.

*   a building no longer comes within the exemptions in Schedule 2 to the Building Regulations where previously it did.

*   a building which contains at least one dwelling contains a greater or lesser number of dwellings than it did previously.

*   a building contains a room for residential purposes where previously it did not.

*   a building which contains at least one room for residential puposes contains a greater or lesser number of such rooms than it did previously.

*   a building is used as a shop where previously it was not.

Parts J1 to J3 will apply to all the material changes of use mentioned above which means that whenever such changes occur the building must be brought up to the standards required by Parts J1 to J3.

Historic buildings

Buildings included in the schedule of monuments maintained under section 1 of the Ancient Monuments and Archaeological Areas Act 1979 are exempt from compliance with the requirements of the Building Regulations.

There are other classes of buildings where special consideration may be needed in deciding what is adequate provision for compliance with Part J:

a. listed buildings;

b. buildings situated in designated conservation areas;

c. buildings which are of architectural or historic interest and which are referred to as a material consideration in a local authority's development plan; and

d. buildings of architectural and historical interest within national parks, areas of outstanding or natural beauty and world heritage sites.

It would not normally be considered appropriate to relax the requirements of Part J since they relate to health and safety. However, it may be necessary to seek alternative technical solutions to those set out in this approved document in order to achieve reasonable standards of safety without prejudicing the character of the host building or increasing the risk of long-term deterioration of the building's fabric or fittings.

In determining what is appropriate in the circumstances, the advice of the local authority's conservation officer should be sought. The views of the conservation officer are particularly important where building work requires planning permission and/or listed building consent.

Notification of work

In almost all cases of new building work it will be necessary to notify a Building Control Body (BCB) in advance of any work starting. There are two exceptions to this: where work is carried out under a self-certification scheme listed in Schedule 2A, and where work is listed in Schedule 2B to the Building Regulations as being not notifiable.

Competent person self-certification schemes under Schedule 2A

Under regulation 12(5) of the Building Regulations it is not necessary to notify a BCB in advance of work which is covered by this Approved Document if that work is of a type set out in column 1 of Schedule 2A to the Regulations and is carried out by a person registered with a relevant self-certification (competent persons) scheme as set out in column 2 of that Schedule. In order to join such a scheme a person must demonstrate competence to carry out the type of work the scheme covers, and also the ability to comply with all relevant requirements in the Building Regulations.

There are a number of schemes authorised for the installation of combustion appliances. Details of current schemes including those

relating to combustion appliances can be found from www.communities.gov.uk/ planningandbuildingregulations/ competentpersonsschemes. Full details of the schemes can be found on the individual scheme websites.

Where work is carried out by a person registered with a competent person scheme, regulation 16A of the Building Regulations and regulation 11A of the Building (Approved Inspectors etc.) Regulations 2000 require that the occupier of the building be given, within 30 days of the completion of the work, a certificate confirming that the work complies with all applicable Building Regulation requirements. There is a also requirement that the BCB be given a notice that this has been done, or a copy of the certificate, again within 30 days of the completion of the work. These certificates and notices are usually made available through the scheme operator.

BCBs are authorised to accept these certificates as evidence of compliance with the requirements of the Building Regulations. However, local authority inspection and enforcement powers remain unaffected, although they are normally used only in response to a complaint that work does not comply.

Work which is not notifiable under Schedule 2B

Schedule 2B to the Building Regulations sets out types of work where there is no requirement to notify a BCB that work is to be carried out. These types of work are mainly of a minor nature where there is no significant risk to health, safety, water efficiency or energy efficiency. Health, safety, and energy efficiency requirements continue to apply to these types of work; only the need to notify a BCB has been removed.

Where only non-notifiable work as set out in Schedule 2B is carried out, there is no requirement for a certificate confirming that the work complies with Building Regulation requirements to be given to the occupier or the BCB.

In general, all work on a combustion appliance which is not a repair or maintenance will be notifiable work and Schedule 2B will not apply. However, it might be possible to add a control device to the appliance or to alter its electrical connection under the allowance in this schedule. Local authority building control departments can give advice in cases of doubt.

Exemptions

Schedule 2 to the Building Regulations sets out a number of classes of buildings which are exempt from all Building Regulations requirements, including those in Part J.

Please note that the Gas Safety (Installation and Use) Regulations apply to buildings exempt under the Building Regulations.

Materials and workmanship

Any building work within the meaning of the Building Regulations should, in accordance with regulation 7, be carried out with proper materials and in a workmanlike manner.

You may show that you have complied with regulation 7 in a number of ways. These include the appropriate use of a product bearing CE marking in accordance with the Construction Products Directive (89/106/EEC) as amended by the CE Marking Directive (93/68/EEC)[1] or a product complying with an appropriate technical specification (as defined in those Directives), a British Standard or an alternative national technical specification of any state which is a contracting party to the European Economic Area which in use is equivalent, or a product covered by a national or European certificate issued by a European Technical Approval issuing body, and the conditions of use are in accordance with the terms of the certificate.

You will find further guidance in the Approved Document supporting regulation 7 on materials and workmanship.

Supplementary guidance

The Department of Communities and Local Government occasionally issues additional material to aid interpretation of the guidance in Approved Documents. This material may be conveyed in official letters to chief executives of local authorities and Approved Inspectors and/or posted on the websites accessed through: www.communities.gov.uk/planningandbuilding/buildingregulations/.

Technical Specifications

Standards and technical approvals are relevant guidance to the extent that they relate to health, safety or water efficiency considerations in the Building Regulations. They may also address other aspects of performance such as service ability, or aspects that, although they relate to health and safety, are not covered by the Building Regulations.

When an Approved Document makes reference to a named standard, the relevant version of the standard is the one listed at the end of the publication. However, if this version of the standard has been revised or updated by the issuing standards body, the new version may be used as a source of guidance provided that it continues to address the relevant requirements Regulations. Where it is proposed to work to the new version instead of the version listed at the end of publication, this should be discussed with BCB in advance of any work starting.

The appropriate use of a product, which complies with a European Technical Approval as defined in the Construction Products Directive, (89/106/EEC) should meet the relevant requirements.

Independent schemes of certification and accreditation

Much of the guidance throughout this document is given in terms of performance.

Since the performance of a system, product, component or structure is dependent upon satisfactory site installation, testing and maintenance, independent schemes of certification and accreditation of installers and maintenance firms will provide confidence in the appropriate standard of workmanship being provided.

Confidence that the required level of performance can be achieved will be demonstrated by the use of a system, material, product or structure which is provided under the arrangements of a product conformity certification scheme and an accreditation of installer scheme.

Third party accredited product conformity certification schemes not only provide a means of identifying materials and designs of systems, products and structures which have demonstrated that they reach the requisite performance, but additionally provide confidence that the systems, materials, products and structures actually provided are the same specification or design as that tested or assessed.

Third party accreditation of installers of systems, materials, products and structures provides a means of ensuring that installations have been conducted by knowledgeable contractors to appropriate standards, thereby increasing the reliability of the anticipated performance.

Many certification bodies that approve such schemes are accredited by the United Kingdom Accreditation Service (UKAS).

Building Control Bodies may accept certification of products, components, materials, or structures under such schemes as evidence of compliance with the relevant standard. Similarly Building Control Bodies may accept the certification of installation or maintenance of products, components, materials and structures under such schemes as evidence of compliance with the relevant standard. Nonetheless a Building Control Body will wish to establish in advance of the work, that any such scheme is adequate for the purpose of the Building Regulations.

---

1 Implemented by the Construction Products Regulations 1991 (SI/1991/1620), amended by the Construction Products (Amendment) Regulations 1991 (SI 1991/1620).

Interaction with other legislation

The Workplace (Health, Safety and Welfare) Regulations 1992

The Workplace (Health, Safety and Welfare) Regulations 1992 contain some requirements which affect building design. The main requirements are now covered by the Building Regulations, but for further information see: Workplace health, safety and welfare. Workplace (Health, Safety and Welfare) Regulations 1992. Approved Code of Practice L24. Published by HSE Books 1992 (ISBN 0 7176 0413 6).

The Workplace (Health, Safety and Welfare) Regulations 1992 apply to the common parts of flats and similar buildings if people such as cleaners and caretakers are employed to work in these common parts. Where the requirements of the Building Regulations that are covered by this Part do not apply to dwellings, the provisions may still be required in the situations described above in order to satisfy the Workplace Regulations.

The Clean Air Act 1993

Under the Clean Air Act 1993 local authorities may declare the whole or part of the district of the authority to be a smoke control area. It is an offence to emit smoke from a chimney of a building, from a furnace or from any fixed boiler if located in a designated smoke control area unless an authorised fuel was used. It is also an offence to acquire an 'unauthorised fuel' for use within a smoke control area unless it is used in an 'exempt' appliance ('exempted' from the controls which generally apply in the smoke control area).

Authorised fuels are fuels which are authorised by Statutory Instruments (Regulations) made under the Clean Air Act 1993. These include inherently smokeless fuels such as gas, electricity and anthracite together with specified brands of manufactured solid smokeless fuels. These fuels have passed tests to confirm that they are capable of burning in an open fireplace without producing smoke.

Exempt appliances are appliances (ovens, wood burners, boilers and stoves) which have been exempted by Statutory Instruments (Orders) under the Clean Air Act 1993. These have passed tests to confirm that they are capable of burning an unauthorised or inherently smoky solid fuel without emitting smoke.

More information and details of authorised fuels and exempt appliances can be found on the internet at http://smokecontrol.defra.gov.uk/

Maintenance

The guidance in this Approved Document provides a way of ensuring that combustion appliances can function safely. For combustion appliances to continue to work safely and effectively it is essential that they are adequately and regularly serviced and maintained.

The Requirements J1/J2/J3/J4/J5/J6

This Approved Document, which takes effect on **1 October 2010**, deals with the following Requirements which are contained in the Building Regulations 2000 (as amended by SI 2001/3335).

Requirement	Limits on application

Part J Combustion Appliances and Fuel Storage Systems

Air supply

J1. Combustion appliances shall be so installed that there is an adequate supply of air to them for combustion, to prevent overheating and for the efficient working of any flue.

Requirements J1, J2 and J3 apply only to fixed combustion appliances (including incinerators).

Discharge of products of combustion

J2. Combustion appliances shall have adequate provision for the discharge of products of combustion to the outside air.

Warning of release of carbon monoxide

J2A. Where a fixed combustion appliance is provided, appropriate provision shall be made to detect and give warning of the release of carbon monoxide.

Requirement J2A applies only to fixed combustion appliances located in dwellings.

Protection of building

J3. Combustion appliances and fluepipes shall be so installed, and fireplaces and chimneys shall be so constructed and installed, as to reduce to a reasonable level the risk of people suffering burns or the building catching fire in consequence of their use.

Provision of information

J4. Where a hearth, fireplace, flue or chimney is provided or extended, a durable notice containing information on the performance capabilities of the hearth, fireplace, flue or chimney shall be affixed in a suitable place in the building for the purpose of enabling combustion appliances to be safely installed.

Protection of liquid fuel storage systems

J5. Liquid fuel storage systems and the pipes connecting them to combustion appliances shall be so constructed and separated from buildings and the boundary of the premises as to reduce to a reasonable level the risk of the fuel igniting in the event of fire in adjacent buildings or premises.

Requirement J5 applies only to:

(a) fixed oil storage tanks with capacities greater than 90 litres and connecting pipes; and
(b) fixed liquefied petroleum gas storage installations with capacities greater than 150 litres and connecting pipes, which are located outside the building and which serve fixed combustion appliances (including incinerators) in the building.

Protection against pollution

J6. Oil storage tanks and the pipes connecting them to combustion appliances shall:
    (a) be so constructed and protected as to reduce to a reasonable level the risk of the oil escaping and causing pollution; and
    (b) have affixed in a prominent position a durable notice containing information on how to respond to an oil escape so as to reduce to a reasonable level the risk of pollution.

Requirement J6 applies only to fixed oil storage tanks with capacities of 3500 litres or less, and connecting pipes, which:

(a) are located outside the building; and
(b) serve fixed combustion appliances (including incinerators) in a building used wholly or mainly as a private dwelling, but does not apply to buried systems.

Particular reference should be made to:

Approved Document B for guidance on compartmentation of buildings for fire safety purposes and for appropriate degrees of fire resistance for compartment boundaries.

Approved Document F for guidance on ventilation for health, and provision of extract ventilation using open flued combustion appliances.

J

Section 0: General guidance

Introduction to the provisions

0.1   This Approved Document gives guidance on how to satisfy the requirements of Part J. Although Part J applies to the accommodation of any combustion installation and liquid fuel storage system within the Limits on Application, the guidance in this Approved Document has been prepared mainly with domestic installations in mind, such as those comprising space and water heating systems and cookers and their flues, and their attendant oil and liquefied petroleum gas (LPG) fuel storage systems. Part J does not include specific provisions relating to the storage of solid fuel (including solid biofuel) but the relevant guidance in Approved Document B should be followed.

0.2   The guidance applies to combustion installations having power ratings and fuel storage capacities up to the limits shown in a) to c) below. Guidance which applies generally is given in this section and Section 1. More specific guidance is then given in:

a.   Section 2 for solid fuel installations of up to 45kW *rated output;*

b.   Section 3 for gas installations of up to 70kW net (77.7kW gross) *rated input;*

c.   Section 4 for oil installations of up to 45kW *rated heat output.*

Section 5 gives guidance on requirement J5 for heating oil storage installations with capacities up to 3500 litres and LPG storage installations with capacities up to 1.1 tonne, although there is no size limit on the application of requirement J5. Section 5 also gives guidance on requirement J6, which is limited to installations where the *capacity* of the oil storage tank is 3500 litres or less, serving buildings used wholly or mainly as private dwellings.

0.3   For installations subject to the requirements of part J but outside the scope of this Approved Document, such as incinerators or installations with higher ratings than those mentioned above, specialist guidance may be necessary. However, some larger installations may be shown to comply by adopting the relevant recommendations to be found in the *CIBSE Guide B* and practice standards produced by BSI and IGEM.

Explanation of terms used

0.4   The following definitions have been adopted solely for the purposes of providing clarity in this Approved Document.

1.   An **appliance compartment** is an enclosure specifically constructed or adapted to accommodate one or more combustion appliances.

2.   A **balanced compartment** is a method of installing an open-flued appliance into a compartment which is sealed from the remainder of the building and whose ventilation is so arranged in conjunction with the appliance flue as to achieve a balanced flue effect.

3.   A **balanced flue** appliance is a type of room-sealed appliance which draws its combustion air from a point outside the building adjacent to the point at which the combustion products are discharged, the inlet and outlet being so disposed that wind effects are substantially balanced. Balanced flues may run vertically, but in the most common configuration they discharge horizontally through the external wall against which the appliance is situated.

4.   The **boundary** is the boundary of the land or buildings belonging to and under the control of the building owner. Depending upon the paragraphs of this Approved Document to which it applies, it may be drawn only around the perimeter of the land in question or extended to the centreline of adjacent routes or waterways as shown in Diagram 1.

Diagram 1 **Boundaries in this Approved Document**

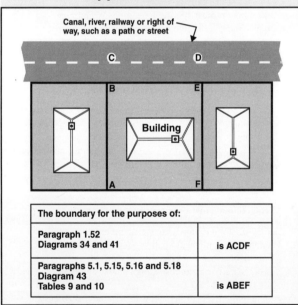

Canal, river, railway or right of way, such as a path or street

Building

The boundary for the purposes of:	
Paragraph 1.52 Diagrams 34 and 41	is ACDF
Paragraphs 5.1, 5.15, 5.16 and 5.18 Diagram 43 Tables 9 and 10	is ABEF

---

5.   A **Building Control Body** is a body that carries out checks for compliance with the Building Regulations on plans of building work and on the building work itself. The Building Control Body may be either the local authority or an Approved Inspector. For further details, see the manual to the Building Regulations.

6.   The **capacity** of an oil tank is its nominal capacity as stated by the manufacturer. It is usually 95 per cent of the volume of liquid required to fill it to the brim.

7. A **chimney** is a structure consisting of a wall or walls enclosing one or more flues (see Diagram 2). In the gas industry, the chimney for a gas appliance is commonly called the flue.

8. A **combustion appliance** (or **appliance**) is an apparatus where fuel is burned to generate heat for space heating, water heating, cooking or other similar purpose. The appliance does not include systems to deliver fuel to it or for the distribution of heat. Typical combustion appliances are boilers, warm air heaters, water heaters, fires, stoves and cookers.

9. The **designation** system in BS EN 1443:2003 expresses the performance characteristics of a chimney or its components, as assessed in accordance with an appropriate European product standard, by means of a code such as EN 1234 – T400 N1 D1 Gxx. Further information is given in Appendix G.

Diagram 2 **Chimneys and flues**

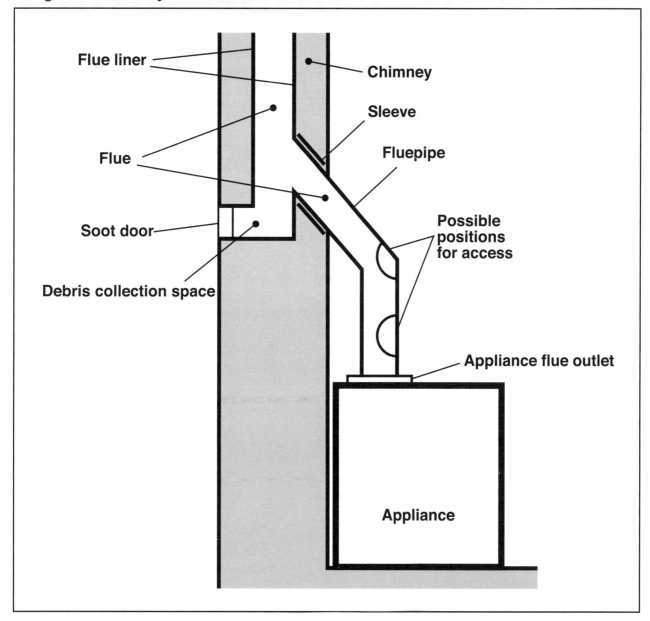

10. A **draught break** is an opening formed by a factory-made component into any part of the flue serving an open-flued appliance. Such openings may be provided to allow dilution air to be drawn into a flue or to lessen the effects of down-draught on combustion in the appliance.

11. A **draught diverter** is a form of draught break intended to prevent conditions in the main length of flue from interfering with the combustion performance of an open-flued appliance (see Diagram 3(a)). It allows the appliance to operate without interference from down-draughts that may occur in adverse wind conditions and excessive draught.

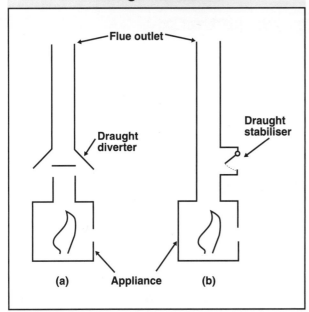

Diagram 3 **Draught diverter and draught stabiliser**

Flue outlet

Draught diverter

Draught stabiliser

(a) Appliance (b)

12. A **draught stabiliser** is a factory-made counter-balanced flap device admitting air to the flue, from the same space as the combustion air, to prevent excessive variations in the draught (see Diagram 3(b)). It is usual for these to be in the fluepipe or chimney, but they may be located on the appliance.

13. **Equivalent area** is defined in BS EN 13141 -1:2004 as the area of a sharp-edged circular orifice which would pass the same air flow rate at the same applied pressure difference as the product or device being tested. The equivalent area of a simple ventilator will be less than the geometrical free area and for complex products may be significantly less.

14. **Factory-made metal chimneys** (also known as system chimneys) are prefabricated chimneys that are commonly manufactured as sets of components for assembly on site (although they can be supplied as one unit), having the performance appropriate for the intended appliance. They are available in various materials and types ranging from single-walled metal chimneys suitable for some gas appliances to twin-walled chimneys with insulation sandwiched between an inner liner and an outer metal wall which are designed for oil or solid fuel use.

15. In a **fanned draught** installation, the proper discharge of the flue gases depends upon the operation of a fan, which may be separately installed in the flue or may be an integral part of the combustion appliance. Fans in combustion appliances either may extract flue gases from the combustion chamber or may cause the flue gases to be displaced from the combustion chamber if the fan is supplying it with air for combustion. Appliances with fans providing the combustion air (including most oil-fired and many gas-fired boilers) are also commonly referred to as forced draught appliances (see Diagram 4). Flues in fanned draught installations run horizontally or vertically and can be at higher or lower pressures than their surroundings, dependent upon the location of the fan.

16. A **fire compartment** is a building or part of a building comprising one or more rooms, spaces or storeys constructed to prevent the spread of fire to or from another part of the same building or an adjoining building. (A roof-space above the top storey of a fire compartment is included in that fire compartment.) A **separated part** of a building is a form of compartmentation in which part of a building is separated from another part of the same building by a compartment wall. Such walls run the full height of the part and are in one vertical plane. Further information on this is given in Approved Document B Vol 2 (see Section 8 Compartmentation and Appendix C Methods of Measurement).

17. A **fireplace recess** is a structural opening (sometimes called a builder's opening) formed in a wall or in a chimney breast, from which a chimney leads and which has a hearth at its base. Simple structural openings (Diagram 5(a)) are suitable for closed appliances such as stoves, cookers or boilers, but gathers (Diagram 5(b)) are necessary for accommodating open fires. Fireplace recesses are often lined with firebacks to accommodate inset open fires (Diagram 5(c)). Lining components and decorative treatments fitted around openings reduce the opening area. It is the finished fireplace opening area which determines the size of flue required for an open fire in such a recess.

18. The **fire resistance** of a component or construction is a measure of its ability to withstand the effects of fire in one or more ways for a stated period of time. Guidance on determination of performance in terms of fire resistance is given in Approved Document B (Fire Safety).

19. A **fire wall** is a means of shielding a fuel tank from the thermal radiation from a fire. For LPG tanks, it also ensures that gas accidentally leaking from the tank or fittings must travel by a longer path and therefore disperse safely, before reaching a hazard such as an opening in a building, a boundary or other potential ignition source.

20. A **flue** is a passage that conveys the products of combustion from an appliance to the outside air (see Diagram 2).

21. **Flueblock chimney** systems consist of a set of factory-made components, made from precast concrete, clay or other masonry units, that are designed for assembly on site to provide a complete chimney having the performance appropriate for the intended appliance. There are two types of common systems, one being solely for use with gas-burning appliances and the other, often called chimney block systems, being primarily designed for solid fuel-burning appliances.

Diagram 4 **Types of installation**

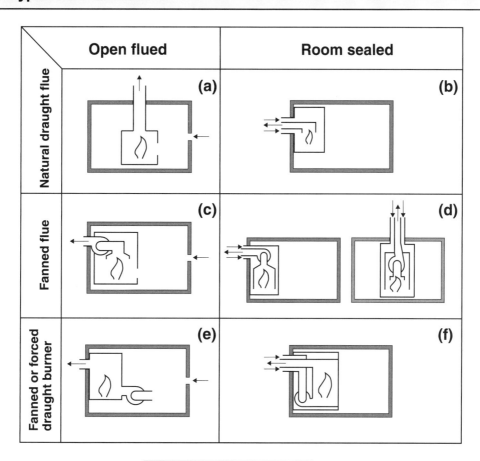

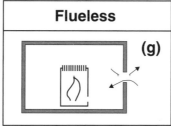

Note – For gas appliances only: CEN TR1749 classifies gas appliances according to their method of evacuating the products of combustion:

Type A – Flueless appliances

Type B – Open flued

Type C – Room sealed

The letters A, B and C are further qualified by numbers to identify the existence and mode of use of fans and draught diverters, as applicable (e.g. B_{11} for an open-flued natural draught appliance with draught diverter).

Diagram 5 **Fireplace recesses**

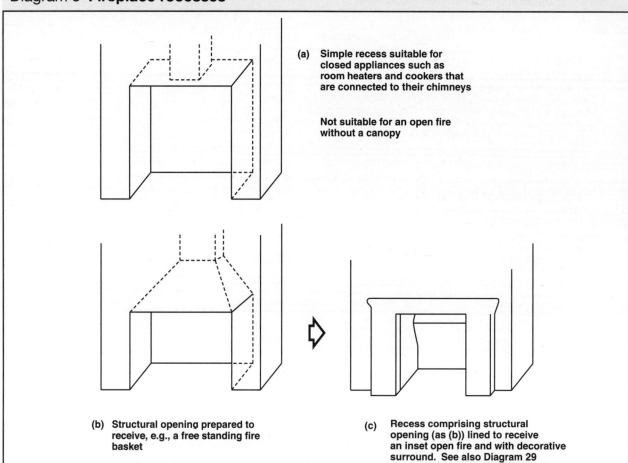

(a) Simple recess suitable for closed appliances such as room heaters and cookers that are connected to their chimneys

Not suitable for an open fire without a canopy

(b) Structural opening prepared to receive, e.g., a free standing fire basket

(c) Recess comprising structural opening (as (b)) lined to receive an inset open fire and with decorative surround. See also Diagram 29

22. A **flue box** is a factory made unit, usually made of metal, which is similar to a prefabricated appliance chamber except that it is designed to accommodate a gas burning appliance in conjunction with a factory-made chimney.

23. A **flueless appliance** is one which is designed to be used without connection to a flue. Its products of combustion mix with the surrounding room air and are eventually transported to the outside as stale air leaves the room (see Diagram 4(g)).

24. A **flue liner** is the wall of the chimney that is in contact with the products of combustion (see Diagram 2), such as a concrete flue liner, the inner liner of a factory-made chimney system or a flexible liner fitted into an existing chimney.

25. A **flue outlet** is the point at which the products of combustion are discharged from the flue to the outside atmosphere, such as the top of a chimney pot or flue terminal.

26. A **fluepipe** is a pipe, either single walled (bare or insulated) or double walled, which connects a combustion appliance to a flue in a chimney. For clarity, when used in this way, it may be called a connecting fluepipe. (Fluepipe is also used to describe the tubular components from which some factory made chimneys for gas and oil appliances are made or from which plastic flue systems are made).

27. A **hearth** is a base intended to safely isolate a combustion appliance from people, combustible parts of the building fabric and soft furnishings. The exposed surface of the hearth provides a region around the appliance which can be kept clear of anything at risk of fire. The body of the hearth may be thin insulating board, a substantial thickness of material such as concrete or some intermediate provision dependent upon the weight and downward heat emission characteristics of the appliance(s) upon it (see Diagram 6).

28. The **heat input rate** is the maximum rate of energy flow into an appliance. It is calculated as the rate of fuel flow to the appliance multiplied by either the fuel's gross or net calorific value.

    Note: Traditionally, the UK has used Gross values, most European standards use Net values. Thus for gas appliances it is now the norm to express this rating as a net value (kW (net)).

29. **Installation instructions** are those instructions produced by manufacturers to enable installers to correctly install and test appliances and flues and to commission them into service.

30. In a **natural draught** flue, the combustion products flow into the flue as a result of the draught produced due to the difference between the temperature of the gases within

Diagram 6 **The functions of hearths**

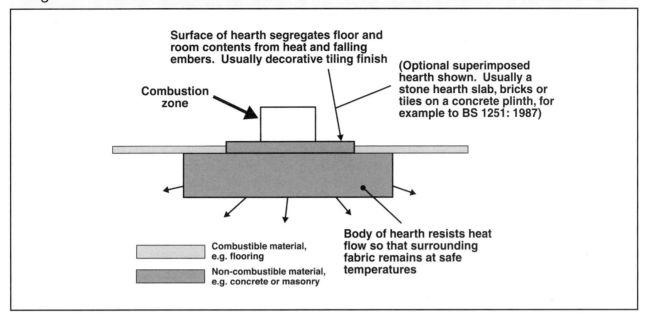

Surface of hearth segregates floor and room contents from heat and falling embers. Usually decorative tiling finish

(Optional superimposed hearth shown. Usually a stone hearth slab, bricks or tiles on a concrete plinth, for example to BS 1251: 1987)

Combustion zone

Combustible material, e.g. flooring

Non-combustible material, e.g. concrete or masonry

Body of hearth resists heat flow so that surrounding fabric remains at safe temperatures

the temperature of the ambient air. Taller flues produce a greater draught at their base. Except for those balanced flue appliances which are designed to discharge directly through the wall adjacent to the appliance, a satisfactory natural draught requires an essentially vertical run of flue (see Diagram 4 (a) and (b)).

31. **Non-combustible material**. This is the highest level of reaction to fire performance. Non-combustible materials include:

    a. any material which when tested to BS 476-11:1982 (2007) does not flame nor cause any rise in temperature on either the centre (specimen) or furnace thermocouples; and

    b. products classified as non-combustible in tests following the procedures in BS 476-4:1970 (2007);

    c. any material classified as class A1 in accordance with BS EN 13501-1:2002 Fire classification of construction products and building elements. Classification using data from reaction to fire tests.

    Typical examples of such materials to be found in buildings include totally inorganic materials such as concrete, fired clay, ceramics, metals, plaster and masonry containing not more than 1 per cent by weight or volume of organic material. (Use in buildings of combustible metals such as magnesium–aluminium alloys should be assessed in each individual case.)

    More detailed information is given in Approved Document B (Fire Safety).

32. A **Notified Body**, for the purposes of the Gas Appliances (Safety) Regulations (1995), means:

a. a body which is approved by the Secretary of State for Trade and Industry as being competent to carry out the required Attestation procedures for gas appliances and whose name and identification number has been notified by him/her to the Commission of the European Community and to other member States in accordance with the Gas Appliances (Safety) Regulations (1995);

b. a body which has been similarly approved for the purposes of the Gas Appliances Directive by another member State and whose name and identification number has been notified to the Commission and to other member States pursuant to the Gas Appliances Directive.

33. An **open-flued appliance** is one which draws its combustion air from the room or space within which it is installed and which requires a flue to discharge its products of combustion to the outside air (see Diagram 4 (a), (c) and (e)).

34. A **prefabricated appliance chamber** is a set of factory-made precast concrete components designed to provide a fireplace recess to accommodate an appliance such as a stove, and incorporates a gather when used with an open fire. The chamber is normally positioned against a wall and may be designed to support a chimney. The chamber and chimney are often enclosed to create a false chimney breast (see also 'flue box').

35. The **rated heat input** (sometimes shortened to rated input) for a gas appliance is the maximum heat input rate at which it can be operated, as declared on the appliance data plate. (See also heat input rate.)

36. The **rated heat output** for an oil appliance is the maximum declared energy output rate (kW) as declared on the appliance data plate.

37. The **rated heat output** for a solid fuel appliance is the manufacturer's declared nominal energy output rate (kW) for the appliance. This may be different for different fuels.

38. A **room-sealed appliance** means an appliance whose combustion system is sealed from the room in which the appliance is located and which obtains air for combustion from a ventilated uninhabited space within the building or directly from the open air outside the building and which vents the products of combustion directly to open air outside the building (see Diagram 4 (b), (d) and (f)).

39. **Solid biofuel** means, for the purpose of this Approved Document, a solid fuel derived from plants and trees. It can include logs, wood chips, wood pellets and other processed plant material.

40. A **throat** is a contracted part of the flue between a fireplace recess and its chimney (see Diagram 22). Throats are usually formed from prefabricated components as shown in Diagram 29.

Measuring the size of flues and ducts

0.5   The size a *flue* or duct (area, diameter etc) should be measured at right angles to the direction in which gases flow. Where offset components are used, they should not reduce the *flue* area to less than the minimum required for the *combustion appliance* (see Diagram 7).

Diagram 7 **Measurement of flues and ducts**

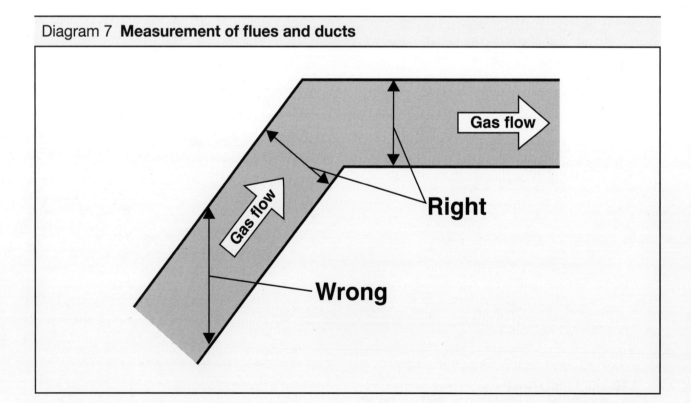

Section 1: Provisions which apply generally to combustion installations

Performance

1.1 In the Secretary of State's view requirements J1 to J4 will be met if the building provisions for the safe accommodation of *combustion appliances:*

a. enable the admission of sufficient air for:

  i. the proper combustion of fuel and the operation of *flues*; and

  ii. the cooling of appliances where necessary;

b. enable normal operation of appliances without the products of combustion becoming a hazard to health.

c. incorporate an appropriate means of warning of a release of Carbon Monoxide for fixed appliances that burn solid fuels;

d. enable normal operation of appliances without their causing danger through damage by heat or fire to the fabric of the building;

e. have been inspected and tested to establish suitability for the purpose intended;

f. have been labelled to indicate performance capabilities.

Note: Whilst, for the purposes of requirement J2A, it is considered appropriate to require carbon monoxide alarms only with solid fuel appliances, such alarms can still reduce the risk of poisoning from other types of appliance.

Air supply for combustion appliances

1.2 *Combustion appliances* require ventilation to supply them with air for combustion. Ventilation is also required to ensure the proper operation of *flues* or, in the case of *flueless appliances*, to ensure that the products of combustion are safely dispersed to the outside air. Installation of *room-sealed appliances* or those with a directly connected ducted external air supply will minimise ventilation energy losses from the room and the risk of cold draughts. In some cases, *combustion appliances* may also require air for cooling control systems and/or to ensure that casings remain safe to touch (see Diagram 8). General guidance on where it may be necessary to install air vents for these purposes is given below.

1.3 Air vent sizes, which are dependent upon the type of fuel burned, are given in Sections 2, 3 and 4 and are for one *combustion appliance* only. The air supply provisions will usually need to be increased where a room contains more than one appliance (such as a kitchen containing an open-flued boiler and an open-flued cooker).

Permanently open ventilation of rooms

1.4 A room containing an *open-flued appliance* may need permanently open air vents. An open-flued appliance must receive a certain amount of air from outside ('combustion air' in Diagram 8) dependent upon its type and rating. Infiltration through the building fabric may be sufficient but for certain appliance ratings and forms of construction, permanent openings are necessary (see Diagram 8).

Permanent ventilation of appliance compartments

1.5 *Appliance compartments* that enclose open-flued *combustion appliances* should be provided with vents large enough to admit all of the air required by the appliance for combustion and proper flue operation, whether the compartment draws its air from a room or directly from outside (see Diagram 8 (b) and (c)).

1.6 Where appliances require cooling air, *appliance compartments* should be large enough to enable air to circulate and high- and low-level vents should be provided (see Diagram 8 (d), (e), (f) and (g)).

1.7 Where appliances are to be installed within *balanced compartments* (see paragraph 0.4(2)), special provisions will be necessary and the appliance and ventilation system manufacturer's instructions should be followed.

Ventilation of other rooms or spaces

1.8 If an appliance is *room-sealed* but takes its combustion air from another space in the building (such as the roof void) or if a *flue* has a permanent opening to another space in the building (such as where it feeds a secondary *flue* in the roof void), that space should have ventilation openings directly to outside. Where the roof-space is to be used as a source of air for a combustion installation serving a dwelling, the dwelling roof ventilation provisions suggested in Approved Document C would normally be satisfactory.

1.9 Where flued appliances are supplied with combustion air through air vents which open into adjoining rooms or spaces, the adjoining rooms or spaces should have air vent openings of at least the same size direct to the outside. Air vents for *flueless appliances*, however, should open directly to the outside air.

Diagram 8 **General air supply to a combustion appliance**
(for sizes see Sections 2, 3 and 4)

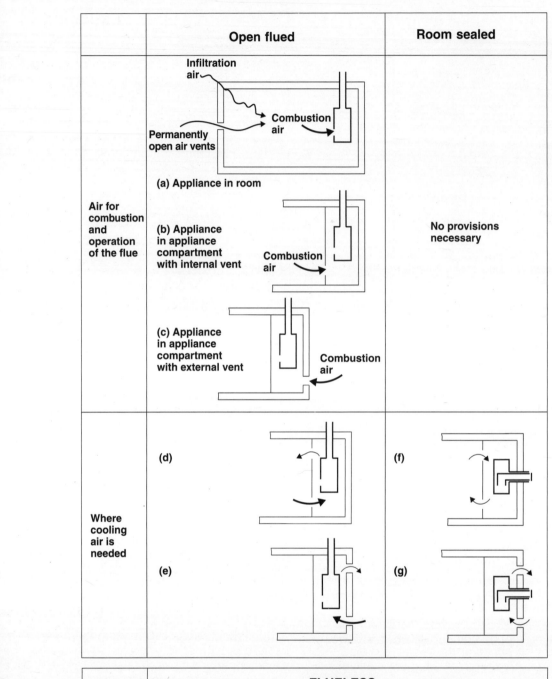

	Open flued	Room sealed
Air for combustion and operation of the flue	(a) Appliance in room — Infiltration air, Permanently open air vents, Combustion air; (b) Appliance in appliance compartment with internal vent — Combustion air; (c) Appliance in appliance compartment with external vent — Combustion air	**No provisions necessary**
Where cooling air is needed	(d); (e)	(f); (g)

FLUELESS

Air for combustion and to carry away its products	(h) Combustion products, Permanently open air vents, Combustion air, Infiltration air

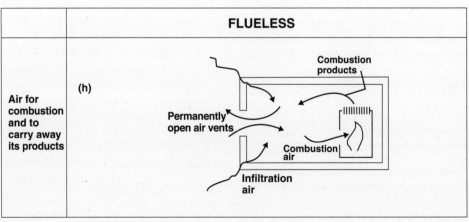

Diagram 9 **Ventilator free areas**

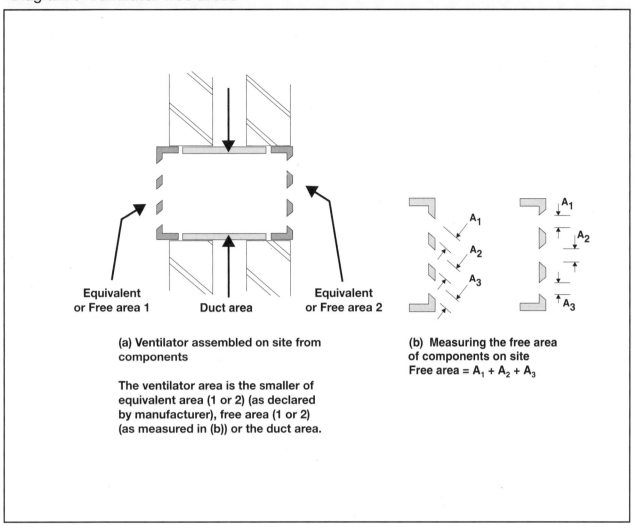

Equivalent or Free area 1

Duct area

Equivalent or Free area 2

A_1
A_2
A_3

A_1
A_2
A_3

(a) Ventilator assembled on site from components

The ventilator area is the smaller of equivalent area (1 or 2) (as declared by manufacturer), free area (1 or 2) (as measured in (b)) or the duct area.

(b) Measuring the free area of components on site
Free area = $A_1 + A_2 + A_3$

Permanently open air vents

1.10 Permanently open air vents should be non-adjustable, sized to admit sufficient air for the purpose intended and positioned where they are unlikely to become blocked. Ventilators should be installed so that building occupants are not provoked into sealing them against draughts or noise. Ventilation openings should not be made in *fire-resisting* walls other than external walls (although they should not penetrate those parts of external walls shielding LPG tanks). Air vents should not be located within a *fireplace recess* except on the basis of specialist advice.

1.11 A way of meeting the requirement would be to size permanently open air vents so that their *equivalent area* is sufficient for the appliance(s) to be installed (taking account where necessary of obstructions such as grilles and anti-vermin mesh), and to site them:

a. outside *fireplace recesses* and beyond the *hearths* of open fires so that dust or ash will not be disturbed by draughts; and

b. in a location unlikely to cause discomfort from cold draughts.

1.12 Where ventilation is to be provided via a single proprietary assembly, for example when it is proposed to use a proprietary ventilator with integral grilles to bridge a cavity wall, the *equivalent area* of the ventilator should be taken as that declared by the manufacturer having been measured by the method in BS EN 13141-1:2004.

1.13 Where two or more components are to be used to provide a non-proprietary assembly, the assembly should be kept as simple and smooth as possible. The assembly should be taken to have an *equivalent area* equal to that of the component with the smallest *equivalent area* in the assembly.

1.14 The *equivalent area* stated in the ventilator manufacturer's literature or marked on the air vent should be used whenever it is available, as this can differ considerably from the free area measured at one end of the air vent. When this is not available the *equivalent area* of a simple ventilator with no internal baffles can be taken as the total unobstructed cross-sectional area, measured in the plane where this area is at a minimum and at right angles to the direction of air flow. For an airbrick, grille or louvre with apertures no smaller than 5mm, it will be the aggregate free area of the individual apertures as shown Diagram 9.

1.15 Grilles or meshes protecting air vents from the entry of animals or birds should have aperture dimensions no smaller than 5mm.

1.16 Discomfort from cold draughts can be avoided by supplying air directly to appliances, locating vents close to appliances (for example by using floor vents), by drawing air from intermediate spaces such as hallways or by ensuring good mixing of incoming cold air by placing external air vents close to ceilings (see Diagrams 10 and 11). In noisy areas it may be necessary to install noise-attenuated ventilators to limit the entry of noise into the building. Transfer or connecting ventilation should be at low level to reduce the transfer of smoke in the event of a fire and otherwise meet the guidance given in Approved Document B.

1.17 Buildings may have air-tight membranes in their floors to isolate them from the ground below. Ventilation ducts or vents installed to supply air to *combustion appliances* should not penetrate these membranes in a way that will render them ineffective. Such membranes (including radon-proof membranes) are described in BRE Report BR 414 (2001) and BRE Report BR 211 (2007), which give guidance when service penetrations are necessary.

Provisions complying with both Part F and Part J

1.18 Rooms or spaces intended to contain open-flued *combustion appliances* may need permanent ventilation to comply with Part J and adjustable ventilation to comply with Part F. Permanently open air vents for *combustion appliances* can be accepted in place of some or all of the adjustable background ventilation for health, dependent upon opening area and location. However adjustable vents installed to meet the requirements of Part F cannot be used as substitutes for the ventilation openings needed to comply with Part J unless they are fixed permanently open.

1.19 Rooms or spaces intended to contain *flueless appliances* may need: permanent ventilation and purge ventilation (such as openable windows) to comply with Part J; and adjustable ventilation and rapid ventilation to comply with Part F. Permanent ventilation provisions to comply with Part J may be acceptable in place of adjustable ventilation provisions for Part F subject to the limitations described in Paragraph 1.18. Openable elements installed for the rapid ventilation of rooms and other provisions made for the rapid ventilation of kitchens, in order to comply with Part F, may be acceptable in place of openable elements for the rapid ventilation of rooms or spaces containing *flueless appliances*.

Diagram 10 **Location of permanent air vent openings, some examples**

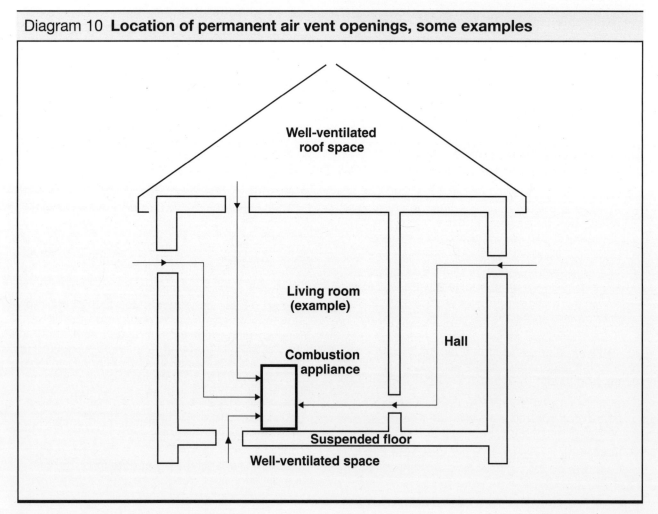

Diagram 11 **Provision of permanent air vent openings in a solid floor**

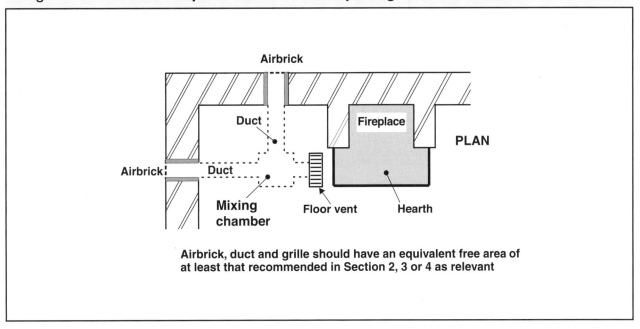

Airbrick, duct and grille should have an equivalent free area of at least that recommended in Section 2, 3 or 4 as relevant

Interaction of mechanical extract ventilation and open-flued combustion appliances

1.20   Extract fans lower the pressure in a building, which can cause the spillage of combustion products from *open-flued appliances*. This can occur even if the appliance and the fan are in different rooms. Ceiling fans produce air currents and hence local depressurisation, which can also cause the spillage of flue gases from *open-flued appliances* or from solid fuel open fires. In buildings where it is intended to install open-flued *combustion appliances* and extract fans, the *combustion appliances* should be able to operate safely whether or not the fans are running. A way of showing compliance in these circumstances would be to follow the installation guidance below, and to show by tests that *combustion appliances* operate safely whether or not fans are running.

a. For gas appliances: where a kitchen contains an open-flued appliance, the extract rate of the kitchen extract fan should not exceed 20 litres/second (72m³/hour).

b. For oil appliances: where a room contains an *open-flued appliance* the extract rate should be limited to 40 litres/second for an appliance with a pressure jet burner and 20 litres/second for an appliance with a vaporising burner.

c. For solid fuel appliances: avoid installing extract ventilation in the same room. An *open-flued appliance* in a kitchen may satisfy the requirements of Part F through passive stack ventilation. Refer to Approved Document F. If mechanical extraction is unavoidable then seek specialist advice to ensure safe operation of the appliance.

d. For commercial and industrial installations, specialist advice may be necessary regarding the possible need for the interlocking of gas heaters and any mechanical ventilation systems.

e. When fans are used to extract radon from below a building follow the guidance in BRE Good Building Guide GBG 25.

1.21   A suitable test would be to check for spillage when appliances are subjected to the greatest possible depressurisation. A prerequisite for this condition is that all external doors, windows and other adjustable ventilators to outside are closed. The depressurisation at the appliance will depend on the particular combination of fans in operation (fans in the room containing the appliance and fans elsewhere in the building) and the pattern of open internal doors, hatches etc. which is established at the time of the test (when fans should be on their maximum useable setting), and the specific combination causing the greatest depressurisation at the appliance depends upon the circumstances in each case. Several tests (which should include a test with the door leading into the room of installation closed and all fans in that room switched on) may therefore be necessary to demonstrate the safe operation of the appliance with reasonable certainty. The effect of ceiling fans should be checked during the tests.

1.22   The presence of some fans may be obvious, such as those on view in kitchens, but others may be less obvious: fans installed in domestic appliances such as tumble dryers and fans fitted to other open-flued *combustion appliances* can also contribute to depressurisation. In addition, fans may also be provided to draw radon gas from the ground below a building (see Paragraph 1.17).

1.23 The appliance manufacturer's *installation instructions* may describe a suitable spillage test for gas appliances but the procedure in BS 5440-1:2008 can be used. For oil-fired appliances the effects of fans can be checked and, where spillage or flue draught interference is identified, it may be necessary to add additional ventilation to the room or space. A flue draught interference test for oil-fired appliances is described in OFTEC Technical Books 2, 4 and 5.

Provision of flues

1.24 Appliances other than *flueless appliances* should incorporate or be connected to suitable *flues* which discharge to the outside air.

1.25 This Approved Document provides guidance on how to meet the requirements in terms of constructing a *flue* or *chimney*, where each *flue* serves one appliance only. *Flues* designed to serve more than one appliance can meet the requirements by following the guidance in BS 5410-1:1997 for oil- and BS 5440-1:2008 for gas-fired systems. However, each solid fuel appliance should have its own *flue*.

Condensates in flues

1.26 *Chimneys* and *flues* should provide satisfactory control of water condensation. Ways of providing satisfactory control include:

a. for *chimneys* that do not serve condensing appliances, by insulating *flues* so that *flue* gases do not condense in normal operation

b. for *chimneys* that do serve condensing appliances:

   i. by using lining components that are impervious to condensates and suitably resistant to corrosion (BS EN 1443:2003 'W' *designation*) and by making appropriate provisions for draining, avoiding ledges, crevices, etc

   ii. making provisions for the disposal of condensate from condensing appliances.

Construction of masonry chimneys

1.27 New masonry *chimneys* should be constructed with *flue liners* and masonry suitable for the intended application. Ways of meeting the requirement would be to use bricks, medium-weight concrete blocks or stone (with wall thicknesses as given in Section 2, 3 or 4 according to the intended fuel) with suitable mortar joints for the masonry and suitably supported and caulked liners. Liners suitable for solid fuel appliances (and generally suitable for other fuels) could be:

a. liners whose performance is at least equal to that corresponding to the *designation* T400 N2 D 3 G, as described in BS EN 1443:2003, such as:

i. clay *flue liners* with rebates or sockets for jointing meeting the requirements for Class A1 N2 or Class A1 N1 as described in BS EN 1457:2009; or

ii. concrete *flue liners* meeting the requirements for the classification Type A1, Type A2, Type B1 or Type B2 as described in BS EN 1857:2003; or

iii. other products that meet the criteria in a).

1.28 Liners should be installed in accordance with their manufacturer's instructions. Appropriate components should be selected to form the *flue* without cutting and to keep joints to a minimum. Bends and offsets should be formed only with matching factory-made components. Liners need to be placed with the sockets or rebate ends uppermost to contain moisture and other condensates in the *flue*. Joints should be sealed with fire cement, refractory mortar or installed in accordance with their manufacturer's instructions. Spaces between the lining and the surrounding masonry should not be filled with ordinary mortar. In the absence of liner manufacturer's instructions, the space could be filled with a weak insulating concrete such as mixtures of:

a. one part ordinary Portland cement to 20 parts suitable lightweight expanded clay aggregate, minimally wetted; or

b. one part ordinary Portland cement to 6 parts Vermiculite; or

c. one part ordinary Portland cement to 10 parts Perlite.

Construction of flueblock chimneys

1.29 *Flueblock chimneys* should be constructed of factory-made components suitable for the intended application installed in accordance with the manufacturer's instructions. Ways of meeting the requirement for solid fuel appliances (and generally suitable for other fuels) include using:

a. flueblocks whose performance is at least equal to that corresponding to the *designation* T400 N2 D 3 G, as described in BS EN 1443:2003, such as:

   i. clay flueblocks at least meeting the requirements for Class FB1 N2 as described in BS EN 1806:2006

   ii. other products that meet the criteria in a).

b. blocks suitable for the purpose lined in accordance with Paragraph 1.27.

1.30 Joints should be sealed in accordance with the flueblock manufacturer's instructions. Bends and offsets should be formed only with matching factory-made components.

Material change of use

1.31 Where a building is to be altered for different use (e.g. it is being converted into flats) the *fire resistance* of walls of existing masonry *chimneys* may need to be improved as shown in Diagram 12.

Connecting fluepipes

1.32 Satisfactory components for constructing connecting *fluepipes* include:

a. cast iron *fluepipes* complying with BS 41:1973 (1998)

b. metal flue pipes appropriately designated in accordance with BS EN1856-2:2004 to suit the appliance and types of fuels to be burnt – refer to detailed guidance in Sections 2, 3 and 4.

c. vitreous enamelled steel pipe complying with BS 6999:1989 (1996)

d. other *fluepipes* having the necessary performance *designation* for use with the intended appliance.

1.33 *Fluepipes* with spigot and socket joints should be fitted with the socket facing upwards to contain moisture and other condensates in the *flue*. Joints should be made gas-tight. A

satisfactory way of achieving this would be to use proprietary jointing accessories or, where appropriate, by packing joints with non-combustible rope and fire cement.

Repair of flues

1.34 It is important to the health and safety of building occupants that renovations, refurbishments or repairs to *flue liners* should result in *flues* that comply with the requirements of J2 to J4. The test procedures referred to in paragraph 1.55 and in Appendix E can be used to check this.

1.35 *Flues* are controlled services as defined in Regulation 2 of the Building Regulations, that is to say they are services in relation to which Part J of Schedule 1 imposes requirements. If renovation, refurbishment or repair amounts to or involves the provision of a new or replacement *flue liner*, it is 'building work' within the meaning of Regulation 3 of the Building Regulations. 'Building work' and must not be undertaken without prior notification to the local authority. Examples of work that would need to be notified include:

a. relining work comprising the creation of new flue walls by the insertion of new linings such as rigid or flexible prefabricated components

---

Diagram 12 **Material change of use: fire protection of chimneys passing through other dwellings**

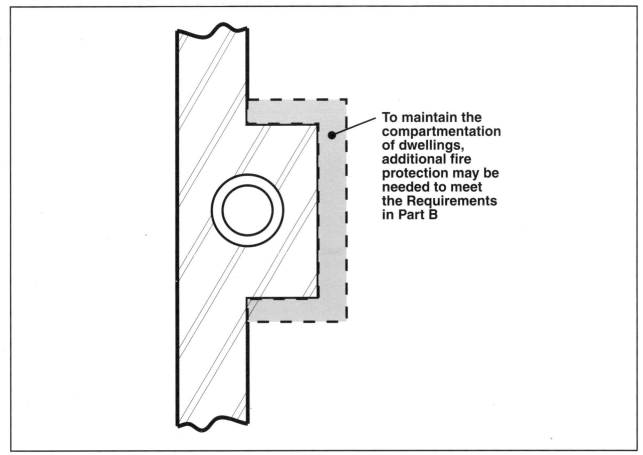

To maintain the compartmentation of dwellings, additional fire protection may be needed to meet the Requirements in Part B

---

b. a cast in situ liner that significantly alters the *flue's* internal dimensions.

Anyone in doubt about whether or not any renovation, refurbishment or repair work involving a *flue* is notifiable 'building work', could consult the building control department of their local authority, or an approved inspector.

Re-use of existing flues

1.36   Where it is proposed to bring a *flue* in an existing *chimney* back into use or to re-use a *flue* with a different type or rating of appliance, the *flue* and the *chimney* should be checked and, if necessary, altered to ensure that they satisfy the requirements for the proposed use. A way of checking before and/or after remedial work would be to test the *flue* using the procedures in Appendix E.

1.37   A way of refurbishing defective *flues* would be to line them using the materials and components described in Sections 2, 3, and 4 dependent upon the type of *combustion appliance* proposed. Before relining *flues*, they should be swept to remove deposits.

1.38   A *flue* may also need to be lined to reduce the flue area to suit the intended appliance. Oversize *flues* can be unsafe.

1.39   If a *chimney* has been relined in the past using a metal lining system and the appliance is being replaced, the metal liner should also be replaced unless the metal liner can be proven to be recently installed and can be seen to be in good condition.

Use of flexible metal flue liners for the relining of chimneys

1.40   A way of relining a *chimney* would be to use a flexible metal *flue liner*, appropriately designated in accordance with BS EN1856-2:2004 to suit the appliance, fuel and flue gas characteristics. Flexible *flue liners* should be used only to reline a *chimney* and should not be used as the primary liner of a new *chimney*. They can be used to connect gas back boilers to *chimneys* where the appliance is located in a *fireplace recess*.

Use of plastic fluepipe systems

1.41   A way of using plastic flue systems and liners would be to use a plastic *flue*, appropriately designated in accordance with BS EN 14471:2005 to suite the appliance, fuel and *flue* characteristics. Plastic fluepipe systems can be acceptable in some cases, for example with condensing boiler installations, where the *fluepipes* are supplied by or specified by the appliance manufacturer as being suitable for purpose.

Factory-made metal chimneys

1.42   Ways of meeting the requirements when proposing *factory-made metal chimneys* include:

a. using component systems appropriately designated in accordance with BS EN1856-1:2003 to suit the appliance and types of fuels to be burnt and installing them in accordance with the relevant recommendations of BS EN 15287-1:2007;

b. for gas and for oil appliances where flue temperatures will not normally exceed 250°C, using twin-walled component systems (and, for gas, single-walled component systems) appropriately designated in accordance with BS EN1856-1:2003 to suit the appliance and types of fuels to be burnt and installing gas appliances in accordance with BS 5440-1:2008;

c. using any other *chimney* system that is suitable for the intended purpose and installed in accordance with the relevant recommendations in BS EN 15287-1:2007 or BS 5440-1:2008, as appropriate to the type of appliance being installed.

1.43   Where a *factory-made metal chimney* passes through a wall, sleeves should be provided to prevent damage to the *flue* or building through thermal expansion. To facilitate the checking of gas-tightness, joints between *chimney* sections should not be concealed within ceiling joist spaces or within the thicknesses of walls without proper access being provided (see paragraph 1.47).

1.44   When providing a *factory-made metal chimney*, provision should be made to withdraw the appliance without the need to dismantle the *chimney*.

1.45   *Factory-made metal chimneys* should be kept a suitable distance away from combustible materials. Ways of meeting the requirement for *chimneys* designated to BS EN 1856-1:2003 comprise:

a. locating the *chimney* not less than distance 'xx' from combustible material, where 'xx' is defined in BS EN 1856-1:2003 as shown in Diagram 13;

b. where a *chimney* passes through a cupboard, storage space or roof space, providing a guard placed no closer to the outer wall of the *chimney* than the distance in a) above.

1.46   Where a *factory-made metal chimney* penetrates a *fire compartment* wall or floor, it must not breach the fire separation requirements of Part B. See Approved Document B for more guidance but the requirements may be met by:

a. using a *factory-made metal chimney* of the appropriate level of *fire resistance* installed in accordance with BS EN 1856-1:2003 Annex NA; or

b. casing the *chimney* in *non-combustible material* giving at least half the *fire resistance* recommended for the *fire compartment* wall or floor.

Diagram 13 **The separation of combustible material from a factory-made metal chimney designated to BS EN 1856-1:2003**

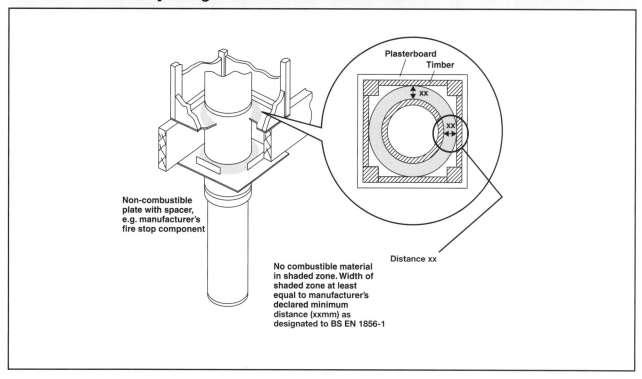

Plasterboard
Timber

Non-combustible plate with spacer, e.g. manufacturer's fire stop component

No combustible material in shaded zone. Width of shaded zone at least equal to manufacturer's declared minimum distance (xxmm) as designated to BS EN 1856-1

Distance xx

Concealed flues

1.47 Where a *flue* is routed within a void, appropriate means of access at strategic locations should be provided to allow the following aspects to be visually checked and confirmed. This is necessary both when an appliance is first installed and subsequently when the appliance is serviced:

- the *flue* is continuous throughout its length

- all joints appear correctly assembled and are appropriately sealed

- the *flue* is adequately supported throughout its length

- any required gradient of fall back to the boiler (required to recover the condensate produced as part of the combustion process) and any other required drain points have been provided.

Means of access for *flues* needs to be sufficiently sized and positioned to allow a visual inspection to be undertaken of the *flue*, particularly at any joints in the *flue*. It is not intended that the means of access should be sized to allow full physical access to the flue system. Diagram 14 shows an acceptable approach for a *flue* in an ceiling void.

Flues should not pass through another dwelling since access for inspection may not always be available to that dwelling and *chimney* system running through it. *Flues* may pass through communal areas including purpose-designed ducts where inspection access is provided.

Any 'means of access' should not impair any fire, thermal or acoustic requirements of the Building Regulations. Refer to the relevant guidance in Approved Documents B, L and E. Where necessary, inspection panels or hatches should be fitted with resilient seals and provide the similar standards of fire, thermal and acoustic isolation to the surrounding structure.

Access hatches should be at least 300mm x 300mm or larger where necessary to allow sufficient access to the void to look along the length of the *flue*. Digram 14 shows an acceptable approach to providing access to a horizontal *flue* located within a ceiling void.

Diagram 14 Example locations of access panels for concealed horizontal flues

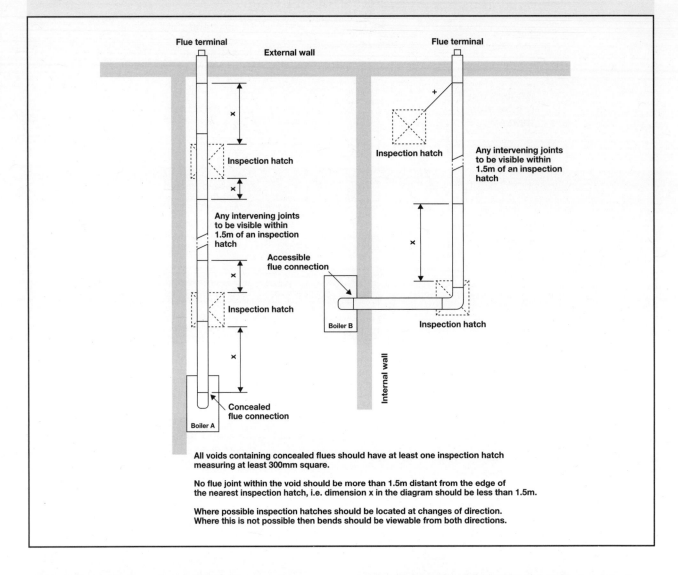

All voids containing concealed flues should have at least one inspection hatch measuring at least 300mm square.

No flue joint within the void should be more than 1.5m distant from the edge of the nearest inspection hatch, i.e. dimension x in the diagram should be less than 1.5m.

Where possible inspection hatches should be located at changes of direction. Where this is not possible then bends should be viewable from both directions.

Configuration of natural draught flues serving open-flued appliances

1.48   Flue systems should offer least resistance to the passage of flue gases by minimising changes in direction or horizontal length. A way of meeting the requirement would be to build *flues* so that they are straight and vertical except for the connections to *combustion appliances* with rear outlets where the horizontal section should not exceed 150mm. Where bends are essential, they should be angled at no more than 45° to the vertical.

1.49   Provisions should be made to enable *flues* to be swept and inspected. A way of making reasonable provision would be to limit the number of changes of direction between the *combustion appliance* outlet and the *flue outlet* to not more than four (each up to 45°), with not more than two of these being between an intended point of access for sweeping and either another point of access for sweeping or the *flue outlet*. (90° factory-made bends, elbows or Tee pieces in *fluepipes* may be treated as being equal to two 45° bends (see Diagram 15)).

Diagram 15 **Bends in flues**

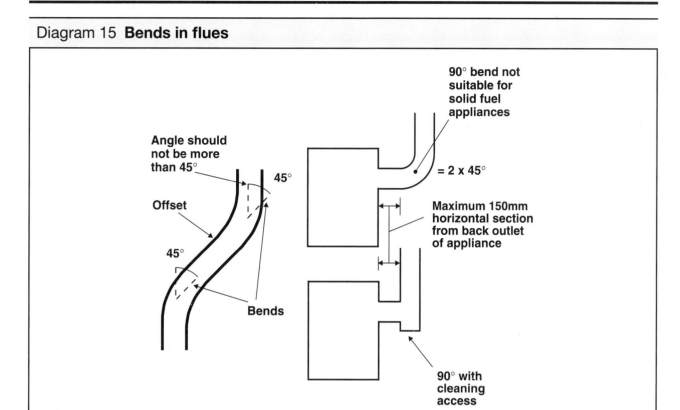

Inspection and cleaning openings in flues

1.50 A *flue* should not have openings into more than one room or space except for the purposes of:

a. inspection or cleaning; or

b. fitting an explosion door, *draught break*, *draught stabiliser* or *draught diverter*.

1.51 Openings for inspection and cleaning should be formed using purpose factory-made components compatible with the flue system, having an access cover that has the same level of gas-tightness as the flue system and an equal level of thermal insulation. Openings for cleaning the *flue* should allow easy passage of the sweeping brush. Covers should also be non-combustible except where fitted to a combustible *fluepipe* (such as a plastic *fluepipe*). After the appliance has been installed, it should be possible to sweep the whole *flue*.

Flues discharging at low level near boundaries

1.52 *Flues* discharging at low level near boundaries should do so at positions where the building owner will always be able to ensure safe flue gas dispersal. A way of achieving this where owners of adjacent land could build up to the *boundary* would be to adopt the suggestions in Diagram 34 or 41, as relevant.

Dry lining around fireplace openings

1.53 Where a decorative treatment, such as a fireplace surround, masonry cladding or dry lining, is provided around a fireplace opening, any gaps that could allow flue gases to escape from the fireplace opening into the void behind the decorative treatment should be sealed to prevent such leakage. The sealing material should be capable of remaining in place despite any relative movement between the decorative treatment and the *fireplace recess*.

Condition of combustion installations at completion

1.54 Responsibility for achieving compliance with the requirements of Part J rests with the person carrying out the work. That 'person' may be, e.g., a specialist firm directly engaged by a private client or it may be a developer or main contractor who has carried out work subject to Part J or engaged a sub-contractor to carry it out. In order to document the steps taken to achieve compliance with the requirements, a report should be drawn up showing that materials and components appropriate to the intended application have been used and that *flues* have passed appropriate tests. A suggested checklist for such a report is given at Appendix A and guidance on testing is given at Appendix E. Other forms of report may be acceptable. Specialist firms should provide the report to the client, developer or main contractor, who may be asked for documentation by the *Building Control Body*.

1.55 *Flues* should be checked at completion to show that they are free from obstructions, satisfactorily gas-tight and constructed with materials and components of sizes which suit the intended application. Where the building work includes the installation of a *combustion appliance*, tests should cover *fluepipes* and [the gas-tightness of] joints between *fluepipes* and *combustion appliance* outlets. A spillage test to check for compliance with J2 should be carried out with the appliance under fire, as part of the process of commissioning to check for compliance with Part L, and (in relevant cases) as required by the Gas Safety (Installation and Use) Regulations.

1.56 *Hearths* should be constructed with materials and components of sizes to suit the intended application and should show the area where combustible materials should not intrude.

Notice plates for hearths and flues (Requirement J4)

1.57 Where a *hearth*, fireplace (including a *flue box*), *flue* or *chimney* is provided or extended (including cases where a *flue* is provided as part of the refurbishment work), information essential to the correct application and use of these facilities should be permanently posted in the building. A way of meeting this requirement would be to provide a notice plate as shown in Diagram 16 conveying the following information:

a. the location of the *hearth*, fireplace (or *flue box*) or the location of the beginning of the *flue*;

b. the category of the *flue* and generic types of appliances that can be safely accommodated;

c. the type and size of the *flue* (or its liner if it has been relined) and the manufacturer's name;

d. the installation date.

1.58 Notice plates should be robust, indelibly marked and securely fixed in an unobtrusive but obvious position within the building such as:

a. next to the electricity consumer unit; or

b. next to the *chimney* or *hearth* described; or

c. next to the water supply stop-cock.

1.59 For *chimney* products whose performance characteristics have been assessed in accordance with a European Standard (EN) and which are supplied or marked with a *designation*, the installer may optionally include this *designation* on the label as shown in Diagram 16.

Access to combustion appliances for maintenance

1.60 There should be a permanent means of safe access to appliances for maintenance. Roof space installations of gas-fired appliances should comply with the requirements of BS 6798:2009.

Diagram 16 **Example notice plate for hearths and flues**

	IMPORTANT SAFETY INFORMATION
Essential information	**IMPORTANT SAFETY INFORMATION** **This label must not be removed or covered**
	Property address .... *20 Main Street* *New Town*
	The hearth and chimney installed in the .... *lounge*
	are suitable for .... *decorative fuel effect gas fire*
	Chimney liner .... *double skin stainless steel flexible, 200mm diameter*
	Suitable for condensing appliance.................... *no*
	Installed on .... *date*
Optional additional information	Other information (optional) .... *Designation of stainless steel liner stated by manufacturer to be T450 N2 S D 3* *e.g. installer's name, product trade names, installation and maintenance advice, European chimney product designations, warnings on performance limitations of imitation elements, e.g. false hearths.*

Section 2: Additional provisions for appliances burning solid fuel (including solid biofuel) with a rated output up to 50kW

Air supply to appliances

2.1 A way of meeting the requirement would be to adopt the general guidance given in Section 1, beginning at Paragraph 1.2, in conjunction with the guidance below.

2.2 Any room or space containing an appliance should have a permanent air vent opening of at least the size shown in Table 1. For appliances designed to burn a range of different solid fuels the air supply should be designed to accommodate burning the fuel that produces the highest heating output.

2.3 Some manufacturers may specify even larger areas of permanently open air vents or omit to specify a *rated output* (for example in the case of a cooker). In these cases, manufacturers' *installation instructions* should be followed subject to any minimum ventilation provisions of this Approved Document.

Size of flues

2.4 *Fluepipes* should have the same diameter or equivalent cross-sectional area as that of the appliance *flue outlet* and should not be smaller than the size recommended by the appliance manufacturer.

2.5 *Flues* should be at least the size shown in Table 2 relevant to the particular appliance, and not less than the size of the appliance *flue outlet* or that recommended by the appliance manufacturer.

Table 1 Air supply to solid fuel appliances

Type of appliance	Type and amount of ventilation (1)
Open appliance, such as an open fire with no throat, e.g. a fire under a canopy as in Diagram 23.	Permanently open air vent(s) with a total equivalent area of at least 50% of the cross sectional area of the flue.
Open appliance, such as an open fire with a throat as in Diagrams 22 and 29.	Permanently open air vent(s) with a total equivalent area of at least 50% of the throat opening area. (2)

Other appliance, such as a stove, cooker or boiler, with a flue draught stabiliser.	Permanently open vents as below:
	 If design air permeability >5.0m^3/(h.m^2) then
	 300mm^2/kW for first 5kW of appliance rated output
	 850mm^2/kW for balance of appliance rated output
	 If design air permeability ≤5.0m^3/(h.m^2) then
	 850mm^2/kW of appliance rated output (4)

Other appliance, such as a stove, cooker or boiler, with no flue draught stabiliser.	Permanently open vents as below:
	 If design air permeability >5.0m^3/(h.m^2) then
	 550mm^2/kW of appliance rated output above 5kW
	 If design air permeability ≤5.0m^3/(h.m^2) then
	 550mm^2 per kW of appliance rated output (4)

Notes:

1. Equivalent area is as measured according to the method in BS EN 13141-1:2004 or estimated according to paragraph 1.14. Divide the area given in mm^2 by 100 to find the corresponding area in cm^2

2. For simple open fires as depicted in Diagram 29, the requirement can be met with room ventilation areas as follows:

Nominal fire size (fireplace opening size)	500mm	450mm	400mm	350mm
Total equivalent area of permanently open air vents	20,500mm^2	18,500mm^2	16,500mm^2	14,500mm^2

3. Example: an appliance with a flue draught stabiliser and a rated output of 7kW would require an equivalent area of: [5 x 300] + [2 x 850] = 3200mm^2

4. It is unlikely that a dwelling constructed prior to 2008 will have an air permeability of less than 5.0m^3/(h.m^2) at 50 Pa unless extensive measures have been taken to improve air-tightness. See Appendix F.

2.6 For multi-fuel appliances, the *flue* should be sized to accommodate burning the fuel that requires the largest *flue*.

Table 2 Size of flues in chimneys

Installation (1)	Minimum flue size
Fireplace with an opening of up to 500mm x 550mm	200mm diameter or rectangular/square flues having the same cross-sectional area and a minimum dimension not less than 175mm
Fireplace with an opening in excess of 500mm x 550mm or a fireplace exposed on two or more sides	See paragraph 2.7. If rectangular/square flues are used the minimum dimension should be not less than 200mm
Closed appliance of up to 20kW rated output which: a) burns smokeless or low-volatiles fuel (2) or b) is an appliance which meets the requirements of the Clean Air Act when burning an appropriate bituminous coal (3) or c) is an appliance which meets the requirements of the Clean Air Act when burning wood (3)	125mm diameter or rectangular/square flues having the same cross-sectional area and a minimum dimension not less than 100mm for straight flues or 125mm for flues with bends or offsets
Pellet burner or pellet boiler which meets the requirements of the Clean Air Act (3)	125mm diameter This may be reduced to no less than 100mm when permitted by the appliance manufacturer and supported by calculation according to BS EN 13384-1:2002. This calculation can be applied to an individual installation or manufacturers can provide precalculated designs.
Other closed appliance of up to 30kW rated output burning any fuel	150mm diameter or rectangular/square flues having the same cross-sectional area and a minimum dimension not less than 125mm
Closed appliance of above 30kW and up to 50kW rated output burning any fuel	175mm diameter or rectangular/square flues having the same cross-sectional area and a minimum dimension not less than 150mm

Notes:

1. Closed appliances include cookers, stoves, room heaters and boilers.

2. Fuels such as bituminous coal, untreated wood or compressed paper are not smokeless or low-volatiles fuels.

3. These appliances are known as 'exempted fireplaces'.

2.7 For fireplaces with openings larger than 500mm x 550mm or fireplaces exposed on two or more sides (such as a fireplace under a canopy or open on both sides of a central *chimney* breast) a way of showing compliance would be to provide a *flue* with a cross-sectional area equal to 15 per cent of the total face area of the fireplace opening(s) (see Appendix B). However, specialist advice should be sought when proposing to construct *flues* having an area of:

a. more than 15 per cent of the total face area of the fireplace openings; or

b. more than 120,000mm² (0.12m²).

Height of flues

2.8 *Flues* should be high enough to ensure sufficient draught to clear the products of combustion. The height necessary for this will depend upon the type of the appliance, the height of the building, the type of *flue* and the number of bends in it, and an assessment of local wind patterns. However, a minimum flue height of 4.5m could be satisfactory if the guidance in Paragraphs 2.10 to 2.12 is adopted. As an alternative approach, the calculation procedure within BS EN 13384-1:2005 can be used as the basis for deciding whether a *chimney* design will provide sufficient draught.

2.9 The height of a *flue* serving an open fire is measured vertically from the highest point at which air can enter the fireplace to the level at which the *flue* discharges into the outside air. The highest point of air entry into the fireplace could be the top of the fireplace opening or, for a fire under a canopy, the bottom of the canopy. The height of a *flue* serving a closed appliance is measured vertically from the appliance outlet.

Outlets from flues

2.10 The outlet from a *flue* should be above the roof of the building in a position where the products of combustion can discharge freely and will not present a fire hazard, whatever the wind conditions.

2.11 *Flue outlet* positions which can meet the requirements in common circumstances are shown in Diagram 17. The *chimney* heights and/or separations shown may need to be increased in particular cases where wind exposure, surrounding tall buildings, high trees or high ground could have adverse effects on flue draught.

Diagram 17 Flue outlet positions for solid fuel appliances

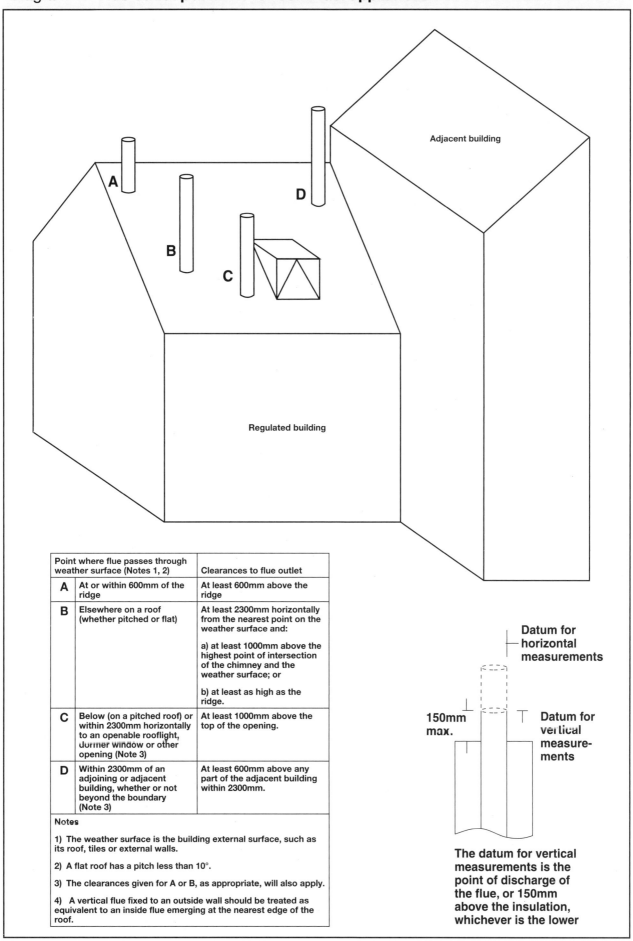

Point where flue passes through weather surface (Notes 1, 2)		Clearances to flue outlet
A	At or within 600mm of the ridge	At least 600mm above the ridge
B	Elsewhere on a roof (whether pitched or flat)	At least 2300mm horizontally from the nearest point on the weather surface and: a) at least 1000mm above the highest point of intersection of the chimney and the weather surface; or b) at least as high as the ridge.
C	Below (on a pitched roof) or within 2300mm horizontally to an openable rooflight, dormer window or other opening (Note 3)	At least 1000mm above the top of the opening.
D	Within 2300mm of an adjoining or adjacent building, whether or not beyond the boundary (Note 3)	At least 600mm above any part of the adjacent building within 2300mm.

Notes

1) The weather surface is the building external surface, such as its roof, tiles or external walls.

2) A flat roof has a pitch less than 10°.

3) The clearances given for A or B, as appropriate, will also apply.

4) A vertical flue fixed to an outside wall should be treated as equivalent to an inside flue emerging at the nearest edge of the roof.

Datum for horizontal measurements

150mm max.

Datum for vertical measurements

The datum for vertical measurements is the point of discharge of the flue, or 150mm above the insulation, whichever is the lower

Diagram 18 **Flue outlet positions for solid fuel appliances – clearances to easily ignited roof coverings**
(Note: This diagram needs to be read in conjunction with Diagram 17)

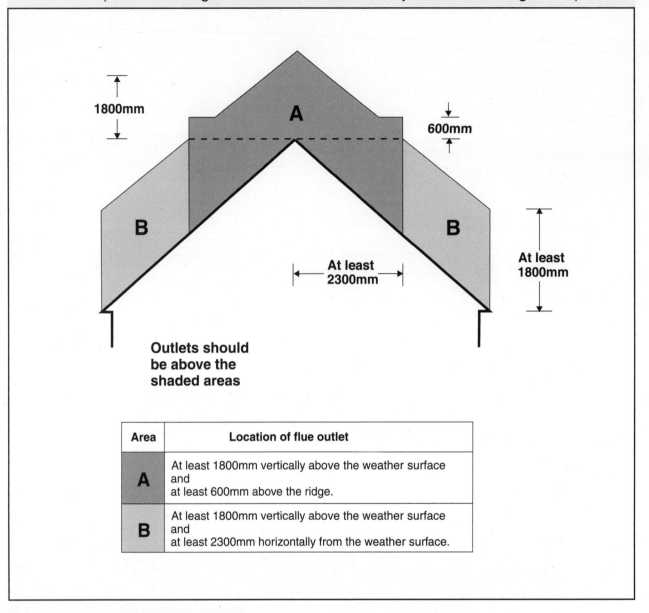

Outlets should be above the shaded areas

Area	Location of flue outlet
A	At least 1800mm vertically above the weather surface and at least 600mm above the ridge.
B	At least 1800mm vertically above the weather surface and at least 2300mm horizontally from the weather surface.

2.12 A way of meeting the requirements where *flues* discharge on or in close proximity to roofs with surfaces which are readily ignitable, such as where roofs are covered in thatch or shingles, would be to increase the clearances to *flue outlets* to those shown in Diagram 18.

Note: Thatched roofs can sometimes be vulnerable to spontaneous combustion caused by heat transferred from *flues* building up in thick layers of thatch in contact with the *chimney*. To reduce the risk it is recommended that rigid twin-walled insulated metal *flue liners* be used within a ventilated (top and bottom) masonry *chimney* void provided they are adequately supported and not in direct contact with the masonry. Non-metallic *chimneys* and cast in-situ *flue liners* can also be used provided the heat transfer to the thatch is assessed in relation to the depth of thatch and risk of spontaneous combustion.

Spark arrestors are not generally recommended as they can be difficult to maintain and may increase the risk of *flue* blockage and *flue* fires.

Further information and recommendations are contained in Hetas Information Paper 1/007 *Chimneys in Thatched Properties*.

Connecting fluepipes

2.13 For connecting *fluepipes* a way of meeting the requirements would be to follow the general guidance in Paragraphs 1.32 and 1.33.

Location and shielding of connecting fluepipes

2.14 Connecting *fluepipes* should be used only to connect appliances to their *chimneys*. They should not pass through any roof space, partition, internal wall or floor, except to pass directly into

Diagram 19 **Protecting combustible material from uninsulated fluepipes for solid fuel appliances**

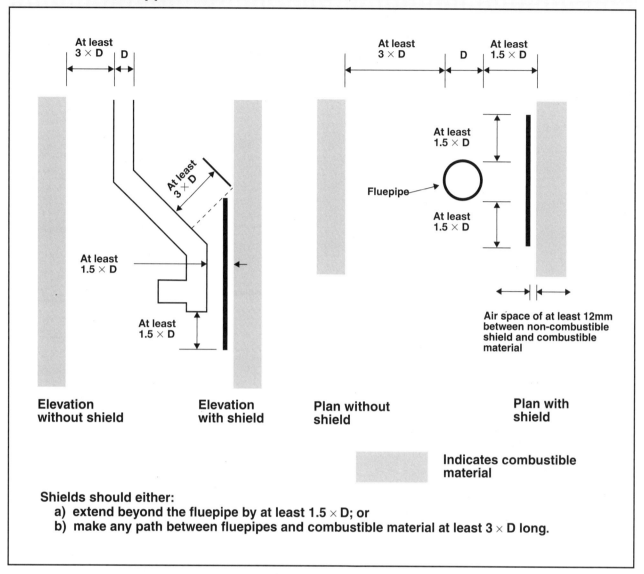

Elevation without shield | Elevation with shield | Plan without shield | Plan with shield

Indicates combustible material

Shields should either:
a) **extend beyond the fluepipe by at least 1.5 × D; or**
b) **make any path between fluepipes and combustible material at least 3 × D long.**

a *chimney* through either a wall of the *chimney* or a floor supporting the *chimney*. Connecting *fluepipes* should also be guarded if they could be at risk of damage or if the burn hazard they present to people is not immediately apparent.

2.15 Connecting *fluepipes* should be located so as to avoid igniting combustible material. Ways of meeting the requirement include minimising horizontal and sloping runs and:

a. following the guidance in Paragraph 1.45 where the connecting *fluepipe* is a factory-made metal *chimney* whose performance is at least equal to *designation* T400 N2 D3 G according to BS EN 1856-1:2003 or BS EN 1856-2:2004, and installed to BS EN 15827-1; or

b. separation by shielding in accordance with Diagram 19.

Debris collection space

2.16 Where a *chimney* cannot be cleaned through the appliance, a debris collecting space which is accessible for emptying and suitably sized opening(s) for cleaning should be provided at appropriate locations in the *chimney*.

Masonry and flueblock chimneys

2.17 Masonry *chimneys* should be built in accordance with Paragraphs 1.27 and 1.28. *Flueblock chimneys* should be built in accordance with Paragraphs 1.29 and 1.30. The minimum *chimney* thickness and distance to combustibles (xxmm) should be no less than the manufacturer's product declaration (Gxx) based on testing to BS EN 1858:2008 (concrete flue blocks) or BS EN 1806:2006 (clay/ceramic flueblocks). Other masonry *chimney* products should exceed the minimum thickness indicated in Diagram 20.

Diagram 20 **Wall thicknesses for masonry and flueblock chimneys**

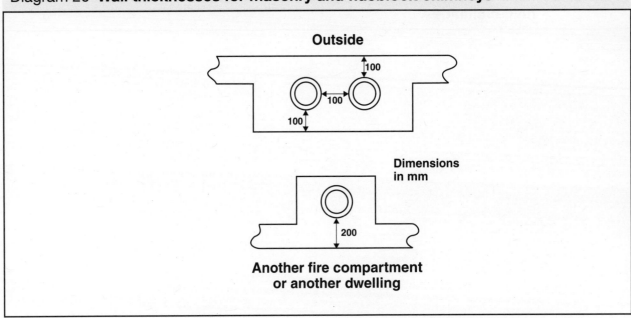

Separation of combustible material from fireplaces and masonry flues

2.18 Combustible material should not be located where it could be ignited by the heat dissipating through the walls of fireplaces or masonry *flues*. A way of meeting the requirement would be to follow the guidance in Diagram 21 so that combustible material is at least:

a. 200mm from the inside surface of a *flue* or *fireplace recess*; or

b. at least xxmm from a flue product with designated separation distance (Gxx); or

c. 40mm from the outer surface of a masonry *chimney* or *fireplace recess* unless it is a floorboard, skirting board, dado or picture rail, mantel-shelf or architrave. Metal fixings in contact with combustible materials should be at least 50mm from the inside surface of a *flue*.

Factory-made metal chimneys

2.19 A way of meeting the requirements would be to comply with Paragraphs 1.42 to 1.46 in Section 1 (but not Paragraph 1.42(b)). The appropriate *designation* is given in Table 3.

Lining and relining of flues in chimneys

2.20 Lining or relining *flues* may be building work and, in any case, such work should be carried out so that the objectives of J2 to J4 are met (see Paragraphs 1.34 and 1.35). Existing *flues* being re-used should be checked as described in Paragraph 1.36. Ways of meeting the requirements include the use of:

a. liners whose performance is at least equal to that corresponding to the *designation* T400 N2 D3 G, as described in BS EN 1443:2003, such as:

 i. factory-made flue lining systems manufactured to BS EN 1856-1:2003 or BS EN 1856-2:2004.

 ii. a cast in-situ flue relining system where the material and installation procedures are suitable for use with solid fuel burning appliances and meeting the relevant requirements of BS EN 1857:2003 + A1:2008.

 iii. other systems which are suitable for use with solid fuel-burning appliances and meeting the criteria in (a).

b. liners as described in Paragraph 1.27.

Diagram 21 **Minimum separation distances from combustible material in or near a chimney**

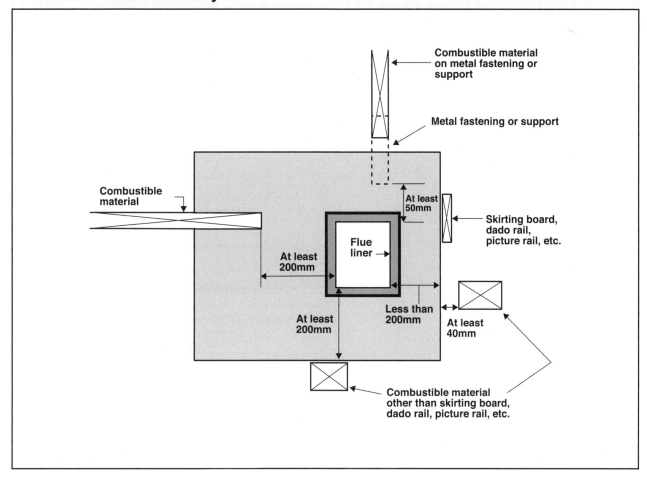

Table 3 Minimum performance designations for chimney and fluepipe components for use with new solid fuel fired appliances

Appliance type	Minimum designation	Fuel type
All solid fuel appliances	Masonry or flueblock flue with liner to T400 N2 D3 Gxx	Coal, Smokeless Fuel, Peat, wood and other biomass
	Clay flue blocks FB1N2	
	Clay/ceramic liners B1N2	
	Concrete liners B2	
	Factory made metal chimneys to T400 N2 D3 Gxx	

See paragraph 1.27–1.29 and 1.42

Formation of gathers

2.21 To minimise resistance to the proper working of *flues*, tapered gathers should be provided in fireplaces for open fires. Ways of achieving these gathers include:

a. using prefabricated gather components built into a *fireplace recess*, as shown in Diagram 22(a); or

b. corbelling of masonry as shown in Diagram 22(b); or

c. using a suitable canopy, as shown in Diagram 23; or

d. using a *prefabricated appliance chamber* incorporating a gather.

Diagram 22 Construction of fireplace gathers

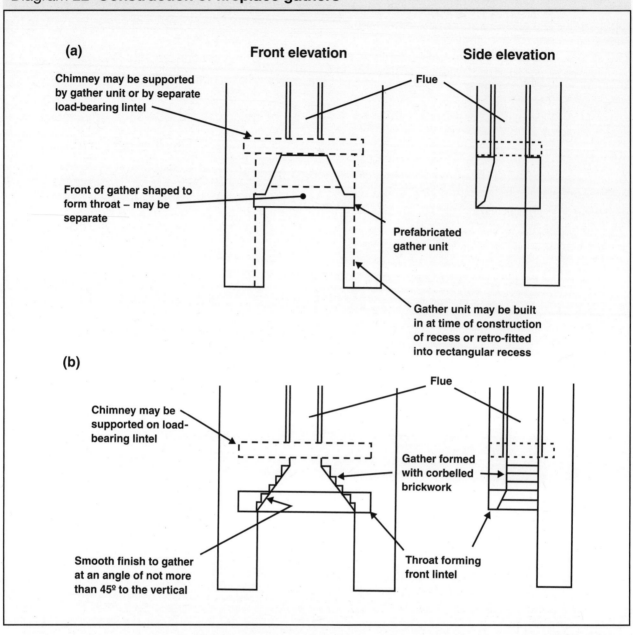

(a)

Front elevation

Side elevation

Chimney may be supported by gather unit or by separate load-bearing lintel

Flue

Front of gather shaped to form throat – may be separate

Prefabricated gather unit

Gather unit may be built in at time of construction of recess or retro-fitted into rectangular recess

(b)

Flue

Chimney may be supported on load-bearing lintel

Gather formed with corbelled brickwork

Smooth finish to gather at an angle of not more than 45º to the vertical

Throat forming front lintel

Diagram 23 Canopy for an open solid fuel fire

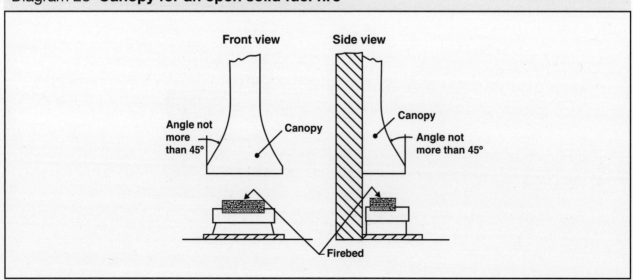

Front view

Side view

Angle not more than 45º

Canopy

Canopy

Angle not more than 45º

Firebed

Hearths

2.22 *Hearths* should be constructed of suitably robust materials and to appropriate dimensions such that, in normal use, they prevent *combustion appliances* setting fire to the building fabric and furnishings, and they limit the risk of people being accidentally burnt. A way of making provision would be to adopt the guidance in Paragraphs 2.23 to 2.28 and to provide a *hearth* appropriate to the temperatures the appliance can create around it. The *hearth* should be able to accommodate the weight of the appliance and its *chimney* if the *chimney* is not independently supported.

2.23 Appliances should stand wholly above:

a. *hearths* made of non-combustible board/ sheet material or tiles at least 12mm thick, if the appliance is not to stand in an appliance recess and has been tested to an applicable appliance standard to verify that it cannot

cause the temperature of the upper surface of the *hearth* to exceed 100°C; or

b. constructional hearths in accordance with the paragraphs below.

2.24 Constructional *hearths* should:

a. have plan dimensions as shown in Diagram 24; and

b. be made of solid, *non-combustible material*, such as concrete or masonry, at least 125mm thick, including the thickness of any non-combustible floor and/or decorative surface.

2.25 Combustible material should not be placed beneath constructional *hearths* unless there is an air-space of at least 50mm between the underside of the *hearth* and the combustible material, or the combustible material is at least 250mm below the top of the *hearth* (see Diagram 25).

Diagram 24 **Constructional hearth suitable for a solid fuel appliance (including open fires)**

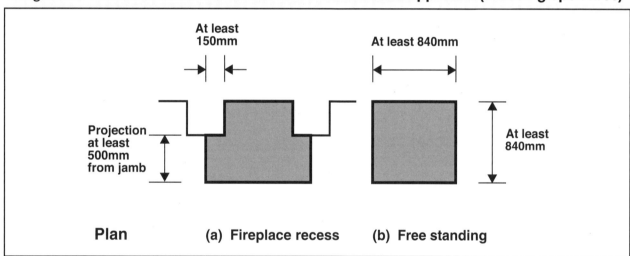

Diagram 25 **Constructional hearth suitable for a solid fuel appliance (including open fires)**

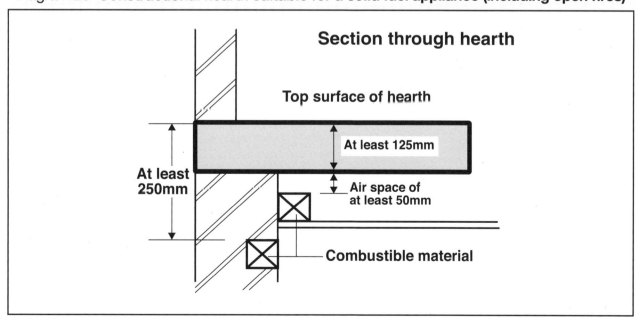

Diagram 26 **Non-combustible hearth surface surrounding a solid fuel appliance**

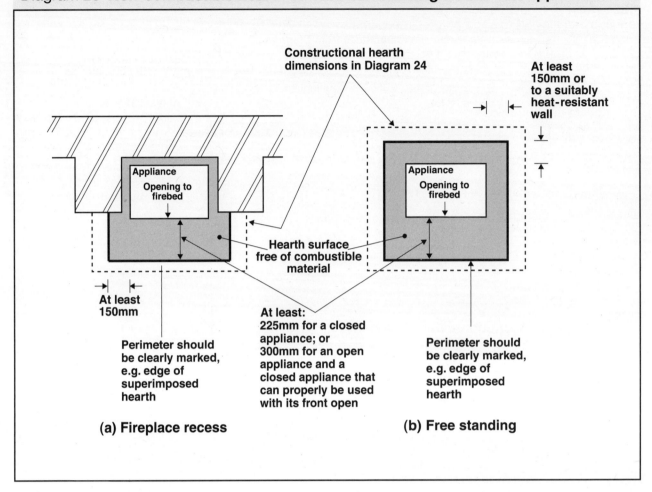

Constructional hearth dimensions in Diagram 24

At least 150mm or to a suitably heat-resistant wall

Appliance
Opening to firebed

Appliance
Opening to firebed

Hearth surface free of combustible material

At least 150mm

**At least:
225mm for a closed appliance; or
300mm for an open appliance and a closed appliance that can properly be used with its front open**

Perimeter should be clearly marked, e.g. edge of superimposed hearth

Perimeter should be clearly marked, e.g. edge of superimposed hearth

(a) Fireplace recess

(b) Free standing

2.26 An appliance should be located on a *hearth* so that it is surrounded by a surface free of combustible material as shown in Diagram 26. This surface may be part of the surface of the *hearth* provided in accordance with Paragraph 2.23, or it may be the surface of a superimposed *hearth* laid wholly or partly upon a constructional *hearth*. The boundary of this surface should be visually apparent to provide a warning to the building occupants and to discourage combustible floor finishes such as carpet from being laid too close to the appliance. A way of achieving this would be to provide a change in level.

2.27 Dimensions shown in Diagram 26 may be reduced to manufacturer's recommendations for appliances with surface temperatures not exceeding 85°C when in normal operation and where there is no risk of spillage of fuel or ash.

2.28 Combustible material placed on or beside a constructional *hearth* should not extend under a superimposed *hearth* by more than 25mm or to closer than 150mm measured horizontally to the appliance.

2.29 Some ways of making these provisions are shown in Diagram 27.

Fireplace recesses and prefabricated appliance chambers

2.30 Fireplaces for open fires need to be constructed such that they adequately protect the building fabric from catching fire. A way of achieving the requirements would be to build:

a. *fireplace recesses* from masonry or concrete as shown in Diagram 28; or

b. prefabricated factory-made appliance chambers using components that are made of insulating concrete having a density of between 1200 and 1700 kg/m³ and with the minimum thickness as shown in Table 4. Components should be supplied as sets for assembly and jointing in accordance with the manufacturer's instructions.

Diagram 27 **Ways of providing hearths**

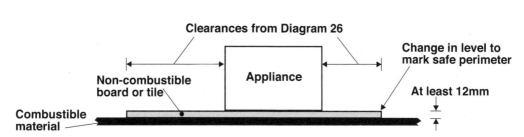

Clearances from Diagram 26

Change in level to mark safe perimeter

Appliance

Non-combustible board or tile

At least 12mm

Combustible material

(a) Appliance that cannot cause hearth temperature to exceed 100°C

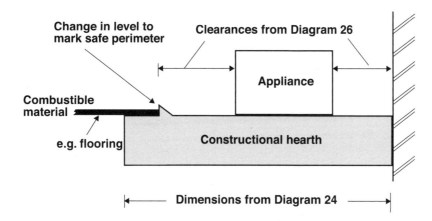

Change in level to mark safe perimeter

Clearances from Diagram 26

Appliance

Combustible material

e.g. flooring

Constructional hearth

Dimensions from Diagram 24

(b) Any appliance standing directly on a constructional hearth

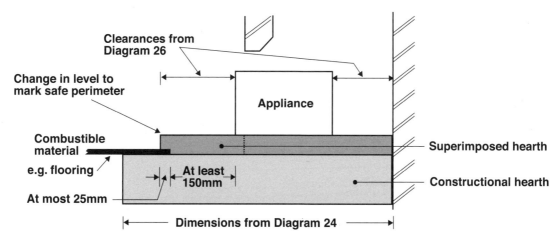

Clearances from Diagram 26

Change in level to mark safe perimeter

Appliance

Combustible material

e.g. flooring

Superimposed hearth

At least 150mm

Constructional hearth

At most 25mm

Dimensions from Diagram 24

(c) Any appliance in a fireplace recess with a superimposed hearth

Diagram 28 Fireplace recesses

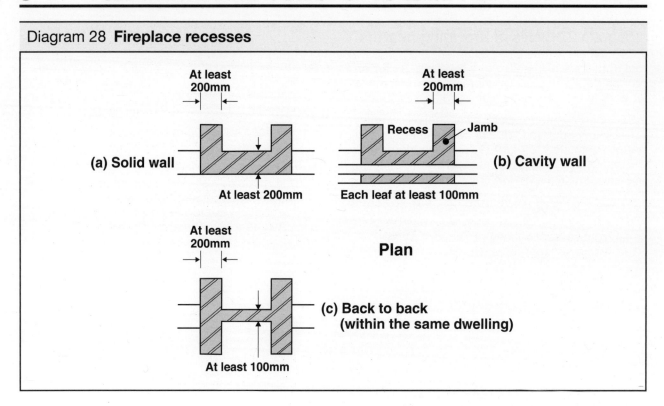

(a) Solid wall
At least 200mm
At least 200mm

(b) Cavity wall
At least 200mm
Recess — Jamb
Each leaf at least 100mm

Plan

(c) Back to back (within the same dwelling)
At least 200mm
At least 100mm

Table 4 Prefabricated appliance chambers: minimum thickness

Component	Minimum thickness (mm)
Base	50
Side section, forming wall on either side of chamber	75
Back section, forming rear of chamber	100
Top slab, lintel or gather, forming top of chamber	100

Fireplace lining components

2.31 A *fireplace recess* may require protection from heat if it is to provide a durable setting for certain appliances such as inset open fires. Suitable protection would be fireplace lining components as shown in Diagram 29 or lining the recess with suitable firebricks.

Walls adjacent to hearths

2.32 Walls that are not part of a *fireplace recess* or a *prefabricated appliance chamber* but are adjacent to *hearths* or appliances also need to protect the building from catching fire. A way of achieving the requirement is shown in Diagram 30. Thinner material could be used provided it gives the same overall level of protection as the solid *non-combustible material*.

2.33 Clearances shown in Diagram 30 may be reduced to manufacturer's recommendations for appliances with surface temperatures not exceeding 85°C when in normal operation.

Alternative approach

The requirements may also be met by adopting the relevant recommendations in the publications listed below to achieve a level of performance equivalent to that obtained by following the guidance in this Approved Document:

a. BS EN 15287-1:2007 Chimneys. Design, installation and commissioning of chimneys. Chimneys for non-room-sealed heating appliances; and

b. BS 8303:1994 Installation of domestic heating and cooking appliances burning solid mineral fuels. Parts 1 to 3.

Carbon monoxide alarms

2.34   Where a new or replacement fixed solid fuel appliance is installed in a dwelling, a carbon monoxide alarm should be provided in the room where the appliance is located.

2.35   Carbon monoxide alarms should comply with BS EN 50291:2001 and be powered by a battery designed to operate for the working life of the alarm. The alarm should incorporate a warning device to alert users when the working life of the alarm is due to pass. Mains-powered BS EN 50291 Type A carbon monoxide alarms with fixed wiring (not plug-in types) may be used as alternative applications provided they are fitted with a sensor failure warning device.

2.36   The carbon monoxide alarm should be located in the same room as the appliance:

a.   on the ceiling at least 300mm from any wall or, if it is located on a wall, as high up as possible (above any doors and windows) but not within 150mm of the ceiling; and

b.   between 1m and 3m horizontally from the appliance.

Note: Further guidance on the installation of carbon monoxide alarms is available in BS EN 50292:2002 and from manufacturers' instructions. Provision of an alarm should not be regarded as a substitute for correct installation and regular servicing.

Diagram 29 **Open fireplaces: throat and fireplace components**

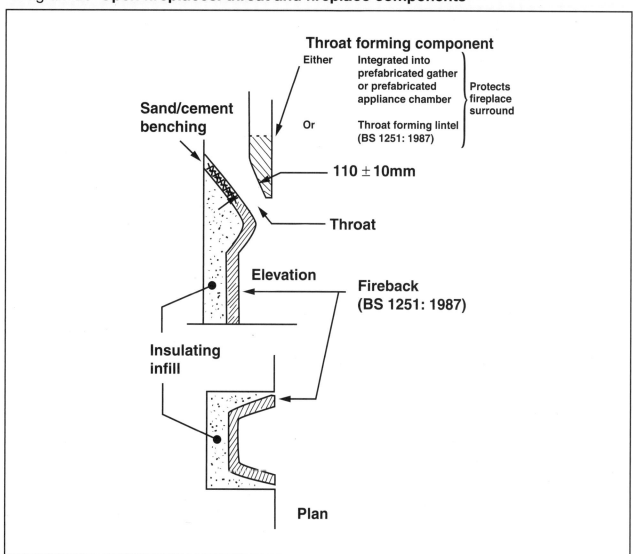

Diagram 30 Wall adjacent to hearths

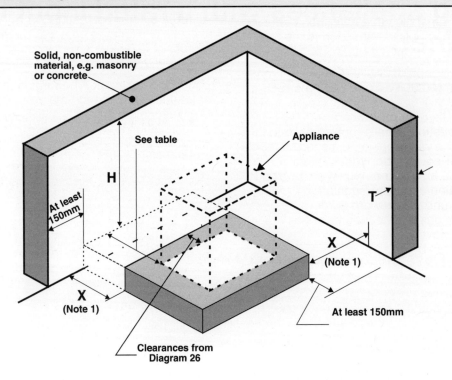

Location of hearth or appliance	Solid, non-combustibe material	
	Thickness (T)	Height (H)
Where the hearth abuts a wall and the appliance is not more than 50mm from the wall	200mm	At least 300mm above the appliance and 1.2m above the hearth
Where the hearth abuts a wall and the appliance is more than 50mm but not more than 300mm from the wall	75mm	At least 300mm above the appliance and 1.2m above the hearth
Where the hearth does not abut a wall and is no more than 150mm from the wall (see Note 1)	75mm	At least 1.2m above the hearth
Note: 1. There is no requirement for protection of the wall where X is more than 150mm.		

Section 3: Additional provisions for gas burning appliances with a rated input up to 70kW (net)

Gas Safety (Installation and Use) Regulations

3.1 All combustion installations must be accommodated in ways that meet the requirements of the Building Regulations. However, gas installations also have to comply with the Gas Safety (Installation and Use) Regulations, which require anyone undertaking gas work to be competent. Any gas engineering business, whether an employer or self employed, must be a member of a class of persons approved by the Health and Safety Executive (HSE). Because of this, the Building Regulations allow that work need not be notified to *Building Control Bodies* if it solely comprises the installation of a gas appliance and it is to be undertaken by a member of such an approved class of persons. The Gas Safety (Installation and Use) Regulations cover the safe installation maintenance and use of gas fittings, appliances and *flues*. The following paragraphs give builders and lay readers an outline of some of the main requirements of the Gas Safety (Installation and Use) Regulations, but for further information reference should be made to the Health and Safety Commission's Approved Code of Practice (see below) or Building Control Bodies.

3.2 The Gas Safety (Installation and Use) Regulations require that (a) gas fittings, appliances and gas storage vessels must be installed only by a person with the required competence and (b) any person having control to any extent of gas work must ensure that the person carrying out that work has the required competence and (c) any gas installation businesses, whether an employer or self-employed, must be a member of a class of persons approved by the HSE; for the time being this means they must be registered with Gas Safe Register.

3.3 Guidance on the individual competency required for gas work is available from the Sector Skills Council Energy and Utility (EU) Skills [http://www.euskills.co.uk/gas]. Persons deemed competent to carry out gas work are those who hold a current certificate of competence in the type of activity to be conducted. Assessment of competence may be through the S/NVQ qualilification under a nationally accredited certification scheme or under the Approved Code of Practice arrangements.

3.4 The Gas Safety (Installation and Use) Regulations control all aspects of the ways combustion systems fired by gas (including natural gas and LPG) are installed, maintained and used, mainly in domestic and commercial premises, and the classes of persons who may undertake gas work. The Regulations may be amended from time to time and whichever Regulations are currently in force at the time an installation is carried out must be complied with. The advice given below reflects the present state of the Gas Safety (Installation and Use) Regulations following the amendments that came into effect on 31 October 1998.

3.5 The text of the Regulations and guidance on how to comply with them are contained in the Health and Safety Executive (HSE) Approved Code of Practice 'Safety in the installation and use of gas systems and appliances'. Important elements of the Regulations include that:

a. any appliance installed in a room used or intended to be used as a bath or shower room must be of the *room-sealed* type;

b. a gas fire, other gas space heater or gas water heater of more than 14kW (gross) *heat input* (12.7kW (net) heat input) must not be installed in a room used or intended to be used as sleeping accommodation unless the appliance is room sealed;

c. a gas fire, other space heater or gas water heater of up to 14kW (gross) heat input (12.7kW (net) heat input) must not be installed in a room used or intended to be used as sleeping accommodation unless it is room sealed or equipped with a device designed to shut down the appliance before there is a build-up of a dangerous quantity of the products of combustion in the room concerned;

d. the restrictions in (a)–(c) above also apply in respect of any cupboard or compartment within the rooms concerned, and to any cupboard, compartment or space adjacent to, and with an air vent into, such a room;

e. instantaneous water heaters (installed in any room) must be room sealed or have fitted a safety device to shut down the appliance as in (c) above;

f. precautions must be taken to ensure that all installation pipework, gas fittings, appliances and *flues* are installed safely. When any gas appliance is installed, checks are required for ensuring compliance with the Regulations, including the effectiveness of the *flue*, the supply of combustion air, the operating pressure or heat input (or where necessary both), and the operation of the appliance to ensure its safe functioning;

g. any *flue* must be installed in a safe position and must be adequate, suitable and effective for use with the appliance which it serves;

h.   no alteration is allowed to any premises in which a gas fitting or gas storage vessel is fitted which would adversely affect the safety of that fitting or vessel, causing it no longer to comply with the Regulations;

i.   LPG storage vessels and LPG-fired appliances fitted with automatic ignition devices or pilot lights must not be installed in cellars or basements.

Diagram 31 **Types of gas fire**

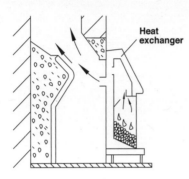

(a) Radiant convector gas fires, convector heaters and fire / back boilers, as described in BS 5871: Part 1

These stand in front of a closure plate which is fitted to the fireplace opening of a fireplace recess or suitable fluebox. The appliance covers the full height of the fireplace opening so that air enters only through purpose-designed openings and the flue gases discharge only through the flue spigot.

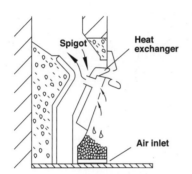

(b) Inset live fuel effect (ILFE) fires, as described in BS 5871: Part 2

These stand fully or partially within a fireplace recess or suitable fluebox and give the impression of an open fire. The appliance covers the full height of the fireplace opening so that air enters only through purpose-designed openings and the flue gases discharge only through the spigot.

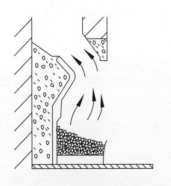

(c) Decorative fuel effect (DFE) fires, as described in BS 5871: Part 3

These are gas-fired imitations which can be substituted for the solid fuel appliances in open fires. Where suitable, they can also be used in flueboxes designed for gas appliances only.

Common designs include beds of artificial coals shaped to fit into a fireplace recess or baskets of artificial logs for use in larger fireplaces or under canopies.

Note: For illustration purposes, this diagram shows gas fires installed at or within a fireplace recess formed by fireplace components within a builder's opening. The actual setting for an appliance depends upon its type and manufacturer's installation instructions.

Gas fires (other than flueless gas fires)

3.6　These appliances fall into the main categories shown in Diagram 31 and the building provisions for accommodating them safely differ for each type.

3.7　Provided it can be shown to be safe, gas fires may be installed in fireplaces which have *flues* designed to serve solid fuel appliances. Certain types of gas fire may also be installed in fireplaces which have *flues* designed specifically for gas appliances. The Gas Appliances (Safety) Regulations 1995 require that particular combinations of appliance, *flue box* (where required) and *flue* must be selected from those stated in the manufacturer's instructions as having been shown to be safe by a *Notified Body*.

Flueless gas appliances

3.8　*Flueless appliances* should meet the requirements, including requirement J2. A way of achieving this would be to follow the guidance on ventilation provisions for *flueless appliances* beginning at Paragraph 3.15.

3.9　A flueless instantaneous water heater should not be installed in a room or space having a volume of less than 5 m³.

Air supply to gas fires and other appliances

3.10　A way of meeting the requirements would be to follow the general guidance given in Section 1, beginning at Paragraph 1.2, in conjunction with the guidance below.

Flued Decorative Fuel Effect (DFE) fires

3.11　Any room or space intended to contain a DFE fire should have permanently open air vents as described in (a) or (b) below, unless the installation is in accordance with Paragraph 3.12:

a.　for a DFE fire in a *fireplace recess* with a *throat*, the air vent *equivalent area* should be at least 10,000mm² (100cm²)

b.　for a DFE fire in a fireplace with no *throat*, such as a fire under a canopy, the air vent should be sized in accordance with Section 2 of this Approved Document, as if the room were intended to contain a solid fuel fire (see Table 1).

3.12　In dwellings with an air permeability greater than 5.0 m³/hr/m² (see Appendix F), permanently open air vents may not be necessary for DFE fires with ratings not exceeding 7kW (net) that have a flue gas clearance rate (without spilling) not exceeding 70 m³/hour.

Flued appliances other than decorative fuel effect fires

3.13　These appliances include inset live fuel effect (ILFE) fires, radiant convector fires and boilers, in both room-sealed and open-flued variants.

3.14　A way of meeting the requirement would be to follow the guidance in Diagram 32. An example calculation illustrating the use of this guidance is given in Appendix C.

Air supply to flueless appliances

3.15　For some *flueless appliances*, it may be necessary to provide permanently open air vents and/or make provision for rapid ventilation as recommended in BS 5440-2:2009 or equivalent, to comply with Part F as well as Part J of the Building Regulations. Some ways of meeting the requirement when installing flueless cookers (including ovens, grills or hotplates), flueless water heaters and flueless space heaters are given in Diagram 33.

3.16　A room containing a gas point intended for use with a *flueless appliance* (such as a gas point for a cooker or a gas point for a space or water heater, the gas point not being adjacent to a *flue*) should have the ventilation provision required for the installation of that appliance (calculated on the basis that an appliance with the largest rating consistent with the table to Diagram 33 could be installed there).

Diagram 32 **Free areas of permanently open air vents for gas appliance installations (other than decorative fuel effect fires or flueless appliances)**

	Open flued	Room sealed
Appliance in a room or space	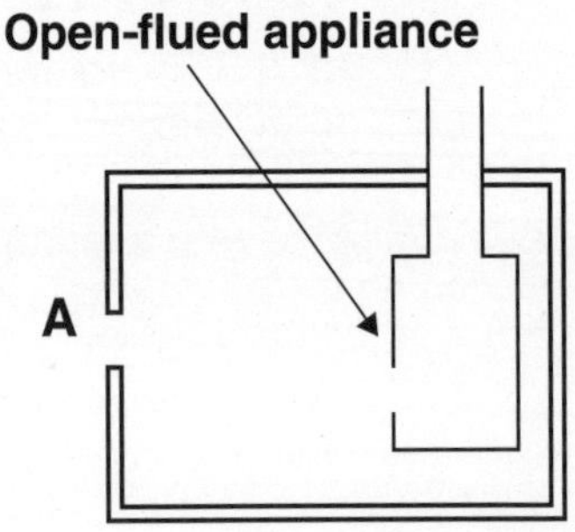 Open-flued appliance A A = 500mm² per kW input (net)	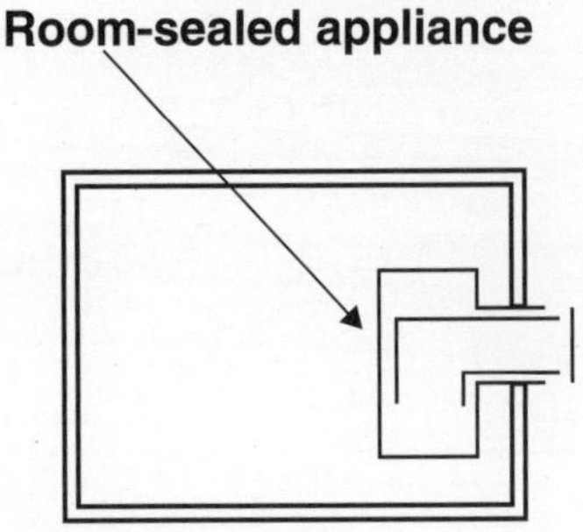 Room-sealed appliance No vent needed
Appliance in an appliance compartment ventilated via an adjoining room or space	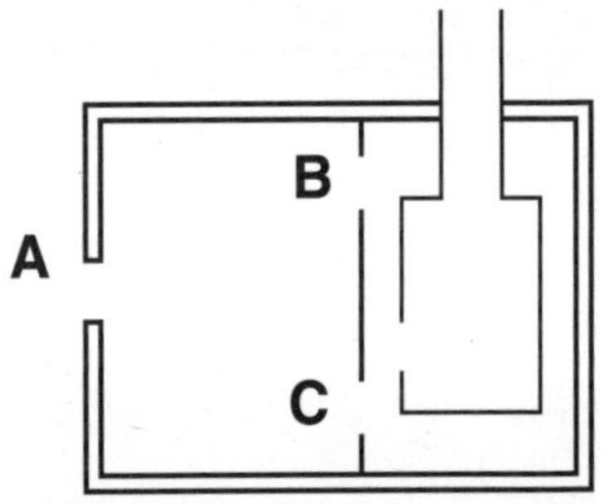 B A C A = 500mm² per kW input (net) B = 1000mm² per kW input (net) C = 2000mm² per kW input	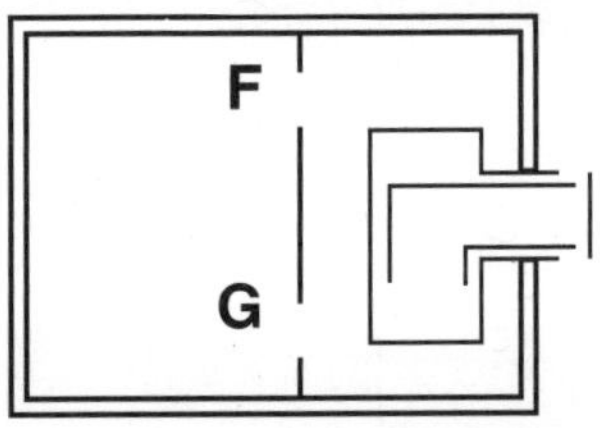 F G F = 1000mm² per kW input (net) G = F
Appliance in an appliance compartment ventilated direct to outside	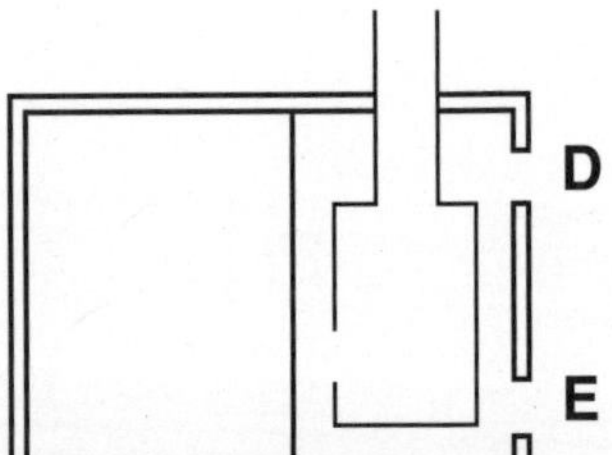 D E D = 500mm² per kW input (net) E = 1000mm² per kW input (net)	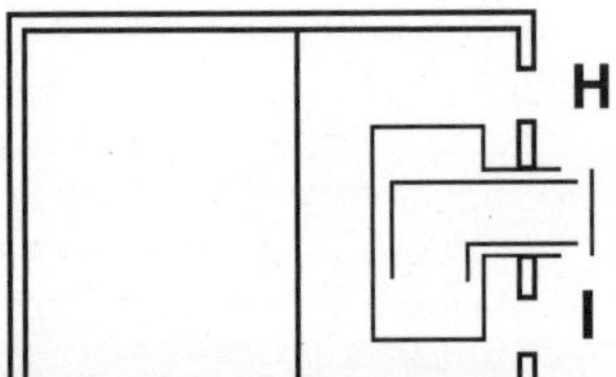 H I H = 500mm² per kW input (net) I = H

Notes:

1. A, D, E, H and I are permanently open vents on the outside. B, C, F and G are permanently open vents between an appliance compartment and a room or a space.

2. Calculations employ the appliance rated net heat input as described in paragraph 0.4.

3. The area given above is the free area of the vent(s) or the equivalent free area for ventilators of more complex design.

4. Divide the area given above in mm² by 100 to find the corresponding area in cm².

5. In older dwellings with an air permeability which is more than 5.0m³/h/m² the first 7kW(net) can be ignored.

Diagram 33 Ventilation for flueless gas appliances

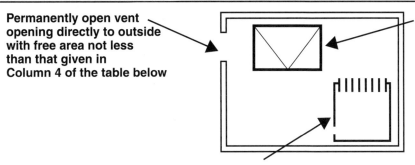

Permanently open vent opening directly to outside with free area not less than that given in Column 4 of the table below

In accordance with Approved Document F:

a) openable window, door or similar form of controllable ventilation opening directly to outside;

or

b) for a kitchen, mechanical extract ventilation

Flueless appliance with a rating not exceeding that given in Column 2 of the table below

Free areas of permanently open air vents			
Flueless appliance type	Maximum appliance rated heat input	Volume of room, space or internal space (m³)	Free area of permanently open air vent (mm²) (3, 4)
Cooker, oven hotplate or grill or combination thereof	Not applicable	<5 5 to 10 >10	10,000 5,000 (8) No permanently open vent needed
Instantaneous water heater	11kW (net)	5 to 10 10 to 20 >20	10,000 5,000 No permanently open vent needed
Space heater not in an internal space (3, 4)	0.045kW (net) per m³ volume of room (5)	all cases	10,000 PLUS 5,500 per kW input (net) in excess of 2.7kW (net)
Space heater in an internal space (3, 4)	0.090kW (net) per m³ volume of internal space	all cases	10,000 PLUS 2,750 per kW input (net) in excess of 5.4kW (net) (7)

Notes:
1. The permanent ventilation provisions listed in this table are additional to the openable elements or (for kitchens only) extract ventilation in accordance with Approved Document F.
2. Divide the area given above in mm² by 100 to find the corresponding area in cm².
3. An internal space here means one which communicates with several other rooms or spaces. An example would be a hallway or landing.
4. For LPG fired space heaters conforming to BS EN 449:2002+A1:2007, follow the guidance in BS 5440-2:2009.
5. No permanently open vent is needed if the room or space has a door direct to outside.
6. Example: for a space heater in a lounge measuring 4m x 4m x 2.4m (= 38.4m³), the appliance rated input should not exceed 38.4 x 0.045 = 1.73kW (net).
7. Example: a hallway containing a space heater with a rated input of 7kW (net) should have a permanently open vent with equivalent area of: 10,000 + 2750 x (7 – 5.4) = 14,400mm².
8. No permanent opening required if the room has a door that opens directly to outside.

Size of natural draught flues for open-flued appliances

3.17 Where builders wish to provide (or refurbish) *flues* for gas appliances but do not intend to supply the appliances, a way of showing compliance would be to size *flues* in accordance with Table 5.

3.18 If an existing *flue* is to be used it should be checked in accordance with Paragraph 1.36.

3.19 For appliances that are CE marked as compliant with the Gas Appliances (Safety) Regulations, *flues* should be sized in accordance with the manufacturer's *installation instructions*.

3.20 Connecting *fluepipes* should be the same size in terms of diameter and/or equivalent cross-sectional area as the appliance *flue outlet*. The *chimney flue* should have at least the same cross-sectional area as that of the appliance *flue outlet*.

Table 5 Size of flues for gas-fired appliances

Intended installation	Minimum flue size	
Radiant / Convector gas fire	New flue: Circular Rectangular	 125mm diameter 16,500mm^2 cross-sectional area with a minimum dimension of 90mm
	Existing flue: Circular Rectangular	 125mm diameter 12,000mm^2 cross-sectional area with a minimum dimension of 63mm
ILFE fire or DFE fire within a fireplace opening up to 500mm x 550mm	Circular or rectangular	Minimum flue dimension of 175mm (1)
DFE fire installed in a fireplace with an opening in excess of 500mm x 550mm	Calculate in accordance with paragraph 2.7 in Section 2	

Note:

1. Some ILFE and DFE appliances require a circular flue of at least 125mm diameter.

Height of natural draught flues for open-flued appliances

3.21 *Flues* should be high enough to ensure sufficient draught to safely clear the products of combustion. The height necessary for this will depend upon the type of appliance, the building height, the type of *flue* and the number of bends in it, and a careful assessment of local wind patterns. For appliances that are CE marked as compliant with the Gas Appliances (Safety) Regulations, compliance with the manufacturer's *installation instructions* will meet the requirements.

3.22 Where an older appliance that is not CE marked is to be installed, a way of showing compliance if it has manufacturer's *installation instructions* would be:

a. for decorative fuel effect fires, to follow the guidance in BS 5871-3:2001 2005; or

b. for appliances other than decorative fuel effect fires, to follow the calculation procedures in BS 5440-1:2008.

Outlets from flues

3.23 Outlets from *flues* should be so situated externally as to allow the dispersal of products of combustion and, if a *balanced flue*, the intake of air. A way of meeting this requirement would be to locate *flue outlets* as shown in Diagram 34 and Diagram 35.

Note: The plume of wet flue products from condensing boilers, positioned in accordance with the safety distances set out in Diagram 34, can sometimes be considered a nuisance for neighbouring properties. Whilst this nuisance is not considered to be within the scope of building regulations, such installations could be considered as a 'Statutory Nuisance' as set out in the Environmental Protection Act. As such installers may wish to adopt the guidance in Chapter 6 of the *Guide to Condensing Boiler Installation Assessment Procedure for Dwellings*

Care may also need to be taken to locate *flue outlets* away from parts of the building that may be damaged by frequent wetting.

Diagram 34 Location of outlets from flues serving gas appliances

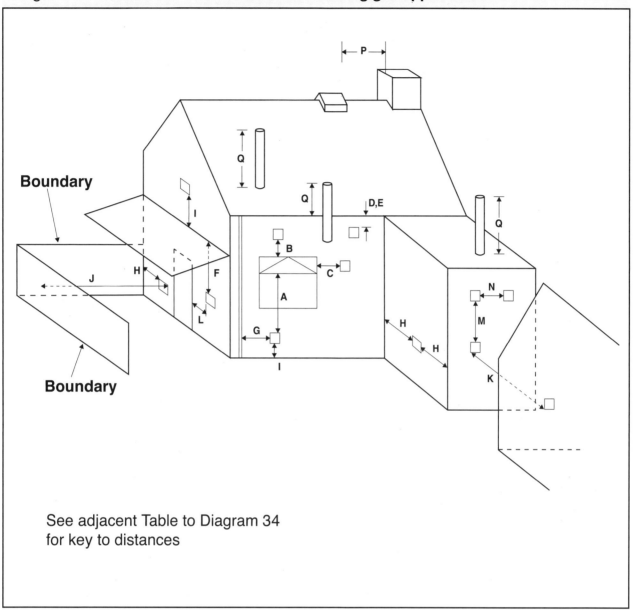

See adjacent Table to Diagram 34
for key to distances

Table to Diagram 34 Location of outlets from flues serving gas appliances

Minimum separation distances for terminals in mm

Location		Balanced flue			Open flue	
		Natural draught		Fanned draught	Natural draught	Fanned draught
A	Below an opening (1)	Appliance rated heat input (net)		300	(3)	300
		0–7kW >7–14kW >14–32kW >32kW	300 600 1500 2000			
B	Above an opening (1)	0–32kW >32kW	300 600	300	(3)	300
C	Horizontally to an opening (1)	0–7kW >7–14kW >14kW	300 400 600	300	(3)	300
D	Below gutters, soil pipes or drainpipes	300		75	(3)	75
E	Below eaves	300		200	(3)	200
F	Below balcony or car port roof	600		200	(3)	200
G	From a vertical drainpipe or soil pipe	300		150 (4)	(3)	150
H	From an internal or external corner or to a boundary alongside the terminal (2)	600		300	(3)	200
I	Above ground, roof or balcony level	300		300	(3)	300
J	From a surface or a boundary facing the terminal (2)	600		600	(3)	600
K	From a terminal facing the terminal	600		1200	(3)	1200
L	From an opening in the car port into the building	1200		1200	(3)	1200
M	Vertically from a terminal on the same wall	1200		1500	(3)	1500
N	Horizontally from a terminal on the same wall	300		300	(3)	300
P	From a structure on the roof	N/A		N/A	1500mm if a ridge terminal. For any other terminal, as given in BS 5440-1:2008	N/A
Q	Above the highest point of intersection with the roof	N/A		Site in accordance with manufacturer's instructions	Site in accordance with BS 5440-1:2008	150

Notes:

1. An opening here means an openable element, such as an openable window, or a fixed opening such as an air vent. However, in addition, the outlet should not be nearer than 150mm (fanned draught) or 300mm (natural draught) to an opening into the building fabric formed for the purpose of accommodating a built-in element, such as a window frame.

2. Boundary as defined in paragraph 0.4 (4). Smaller separations to the boundary may be acceptable for appliances that have been shown to operate safely with such separations from surfaces adjacent to or opposite the flue outlet.

3. Should not be used.

4. This dimension may be reduced to 75mm for appliances of up to 5kW input (net).

   N/A means not applicable.

Diagram 35 **Location of outlets near roof windows from flues serving gas appliances**

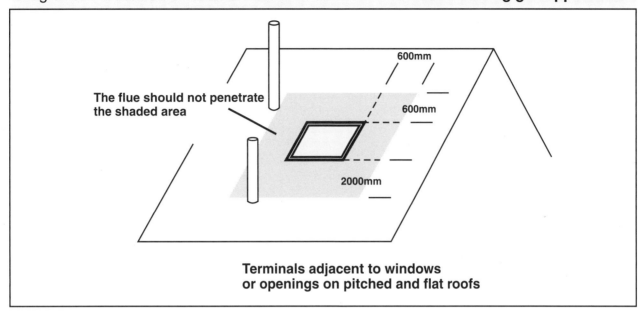

The flue should not penetrate the shaded area

600mm

600mm

2000mm

Terminals adjacent to windows or openings on pitched and flat roofs

3.24 *Flue outlets* should be protected where *flues* are at significant risk of blockage. Guidance on meeting this requirement is given below.

3.25 *Flues* serving *natural draught open-flued appliances* should be fitted with outlet terminals if the flue diameter is no greater than 170mm. Suitable terminals include those appropriately designated in accordance with BS EN 1856-1:2003, and conforming to BS EN 13502:2002. The risk of blockage of *flues* of more than 170mm diameter should be assessed in the light of local conditions. In areas where nests of squirrels or jackdaws are likely, the fitting of a protective cage designed for solid fuel use and having a mesh size no larger than 25mm (but no smaller than 6mm) may be an acceptable provision if the total free area of its outlet openings is at least twice the cross-sectional area of the *flue*.

3.26 A *flue outlet* should be protected with a guard if persons could come into contact with it or if it could be damaged. If a *flue outlet* is in a vulnerable position, such as where the *flue* discharges within reach from the ground, or a balcony, veranda or a window, it should be designed to prevent the entry of any matter that could obstruct the flow of flue gases.

Provision of flues

3.27 Satisfactory provision of *chimneys* and *fluepipes* for gas appliances may be achieved by:

a. following the guidance on the selection of components and the manner of their installation as given in Paragraphs 3.28 to 3.35 and the references to Section 1; or (if the intended appliance is new and of known type)

or (if the intended appliance is new and of known type):

b. i) using factory-made components that achieve a performance at least equal to that corresponding to the *designation* given in Table 6 for the intended appliance type when tested to an appropriate European *chimney* standard (BS EN); and

ii) installing these components in accordance with the guidance in Paragraphs 3.28 to 3.35 and Section 1, as relevant, and in accordance with the appliance manufacturer's and component manufacturer's *installation instructions*.

Table 6 **Minimum performance designations for chimney and fluepipe components for use with new gas appliances**

Appliance type		Minimum designation (see notes)
Boiler: open-flued	Natural draught	T250 N2 D 1 O
	Fanned draught	T250 P2 D 1 O
	Condensing	T140 P2 W 1 O
Boiler: room-sealed	Natural draught	T250 N2 D 1 O
	Fanned draught	T250 P2 D 1 O
	Condensing	T140 P2 W 1 O
Gas fire – radiant/convector, ILFE or DFE		T250 N2 D 1 O
Air heater	Natural draught	T250 N2 D 1 O
	Fanned draught	T250 P2 D 1 O
	SE – duct	T250 N2 D 1 O

Notes:

1. The designation of chimney products is described in Appendix G. The BS EN for the product will specify its full designation and marking requirements.

2. These are default designations. Where the appliance manufacturer's installation instructions specify a higher designation, this should be complied with.

Connecting fluepipe components

3.28 Satisfactory components for connecting *fluepipes* include:

a. any of the options in Paragraph 1.32; or

b. sheet metal *fluepipes* as described in BS EN 1856-2:2004; or

c. fibre cement pipes as described in BS EN 1857:2003+A1:2008; or

d. any other material or component that has been certified as suitable for this purpose.

Masonry chimneys

3.29 Masonry *chimneys* should be built in accordance with Paragraphs 1.27 and 1.28 in Section 1.

Flueblock chimneys

3.30 *Chimneys* can be constructed from factory-made flueblock systems primarily designed for solid fuel, as described in Paragraphs 1.29 and 1.30 in Section 1. They can also be constructed from factory-made flueblock systems comprising straight blocks, recess units, lintel blocks, offset blocks, transfer blocks and jointing materials complying with:

a. BS EN 1858-1:2003 for concrete flueblocks of at least class D2; or

b. BS EN 1806:2006 for clay/ceramic flueblocks with a performance class of at least FB4 N2.

3.31 *Flueblock chimneys* should be installed with sealed joints in accordance with the flueblock manufacturer's *installation instructions*. Where bends or offsets are required, these should be formed using matching factory-made components. Flueblocks which are not intended to be bonded into surrounding masonry should be supported and restrained in accordance with the manufacturer's *installation instructions*.

Factory-made metal chimneys

3.32 *Chimneys* for gas appliances may be constructed using systems described in Paragraphs 1.42 to 1.46 in Section 1. *Factory-made metal chimneys* should be guarded if they could be at risk of damage or the burn hazard they present to people is not immediately apparent.

Location and shielding of flues

3.33 Combustible materials in the building fabric should be protected from the heat dissipation from *flues* so that they are not at risk of catching fire. A way of meeting the requirement would be to follow the guidance in Table 6.

3.34 Where a *fluepipe* or *chimney* penetrates a *fire compartment* wall or floor, it must not breach the fire separation requirements of Part B. See Approved Document B for more guidance.

Table 7 Protecting buildings from hot flues

Flue within	Protection measures
Connecting fluepipe	Flues should be at least 25mm from any combustible material (measured from the outer surface of the flue wall, or the outer surface of the inner wall in the case of multi-walled products). Where passing through a combustible wall, floor or roof (other than a compartment wall, floor or roof) this separation can be achieved by a non-combustible sleeve enclosing the fluepipe or chimney with a 25mm air-space to the relevant flue wall. (The air-space could be wholly or partially filled with non-combustible insulating material).
Factory-made chimney appropriately designated to BS EN 1856-1:2003	
Factory-made chimney appropriately designated to BS EN 1856-1:2003 and BS EN 1856-2:2004	Install in accordance with Paragraph 1.45 of this Approved Document with minimum separation distances according to flue designation.
Masonry chimney	Provide at least 25mm of masonry between flues and any combustible material.
Flueblock chimney	Provide flueblock walls at least 25mm thick.

3.35 Connecting *fluepipes* and factory-made *chimneys* should also be guarded if they could be at risk of damage or if they present a burn hazard to people that is not immediately apparent

Relining of flues in chimneys

3.36 Lining or relining *flues* may be building work and, in any case, such work should be carried out so that the objectives of requirements J2 to J4 are met (see Paragraphs 1.34 and 1.35). Existing *flues* being re-used should be checked as described in Paragraph 1.36. For *flue liners* serving gas appliances, ways of meeting the requirements include the use of:

a. liners as described in Paragraph 1.27;

b. liners as described in Paragraph 2.20;

c. flexible stainless steel liners appropriately designated to BS EN 1856-1:2003 (refer to Table 6);

d. other systems suitable for the purpose.

3.37 Flexible metal *flue liners* should be installed in one complete length without joints within the *chimney*. Other than for sealing at the top and the bottom, the space between the *chimney* and the liner should be left empty unless this is contrary to the manufacturer's instructions. Double-skin flexible *flue liners* should be *installed* in accordance with the manufacturer's installation *instructions*. BS 715 liners should be installed in accordance with BS 5440-1:2008.

Diagram 36 Bases for back boilers (installation using a proprietary back boiler enclosure shown)

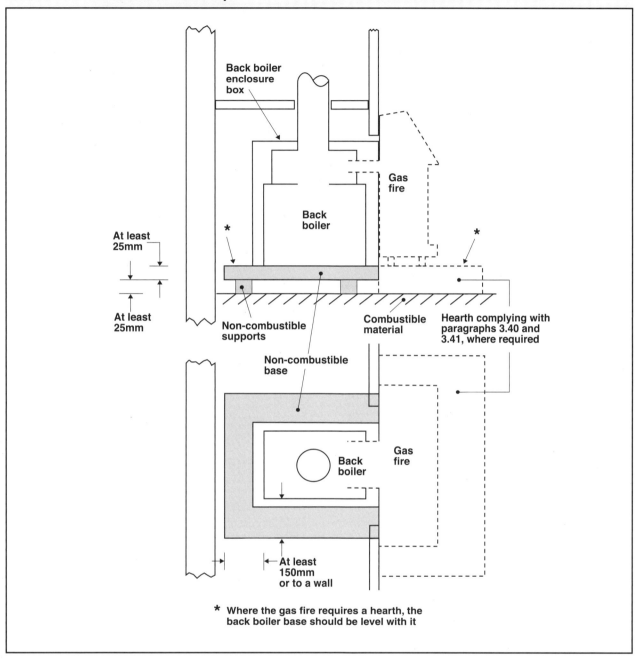

* Where the gas fire requires a hearth, the back boiler base should be level with it

Debris collection space for chimneys

3.38   A debris collection space should be provided at the base of a *flue* unless it is lined, or constructed of flue blocks, or is a *factory-made metal chimney* with a *flue box*. This can be achieved by providing a space having a volume of not less than 12 litres and a depth of at least 250mm below the point where flue gases discharge into the *chimney*. The space should be readily accessible for clearance of debris, for example by removal of the appliance. For gas fires of the type illustrated in Diagram 31 (a) and (b), there should be at least 50mm clearance between the end of the appliance *flue outlet* and any surface.

Bases for back boilers

3.39   Provisions for back boilers should adequately protect the fabric of the building from heat. A way of meeting the requirement would be to stand back boilers on *hearths* intended for solid fuel appliances. Alternatively, unless otherwise stated in the appliance manufacturer's instructions, a way of meeting the requirements would be to stand back boilers on bases complying with Diagram 36.

Diagram 37 **Hearths for decorative fuel effect (DFE) and inset live fuel effect (ILFE) fires: minimum plan dimensions of non-combustible surfaces**

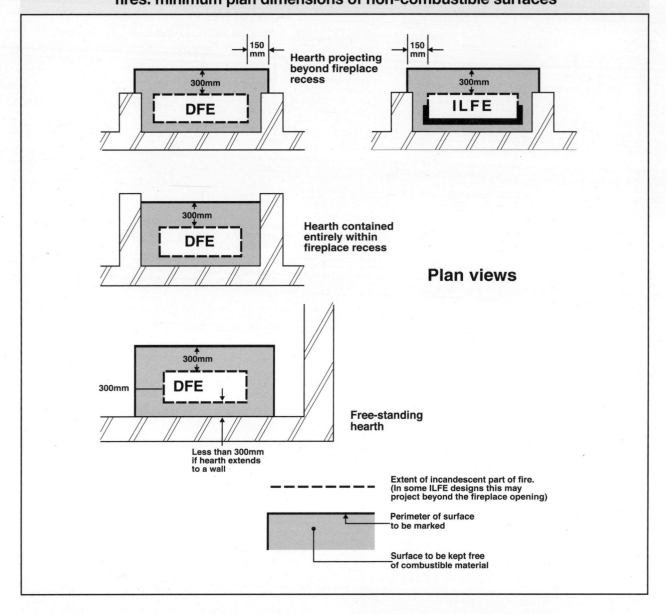

Hearths

3.40 Appliances should be placed on *hearths* unless:

a. they are to be installed so that every part of any flame or incandescent material will be at least 225mm above the floor; or

b. the manufacturer's instructions state that a *hearth* is not required.

3.41 Where *hearths* are required, guidance on their minimum plan dimensions is given in Diagrams 37 and 38. *Hearths* should comprise at least a (top) layer of non-combustible, non-friable material not less than 12mm thick. The edges of *hearths* should be marked to provide a warning to the building occupants and to discourage combustible floor finishes such as carpet from being laid too close to the appliance. A way of achieving this would be to provide a change in level.

Shielding of appliances

3.42 Gas-fired appliances should be located where accidental contact is unlikely and surrounded by a non-combustible surface which provides adequate separation from combustible materials. For appliances that are CE marked as compliant with the Gas Appliances (Safety) Regulations, a way of meeting the requirement would be to adopt the manufacturer's instructions. An alternative approach would be to protect combustible fabric with:

a. a shield of *non-combustible material*, such as insulating board, with a *fire-resistant* surface; or

b. an air space of at least 75mm (see Diagram 39).

Diagram 38 **Hearths for other appliances: plan dimension of non-combustible surfaces**

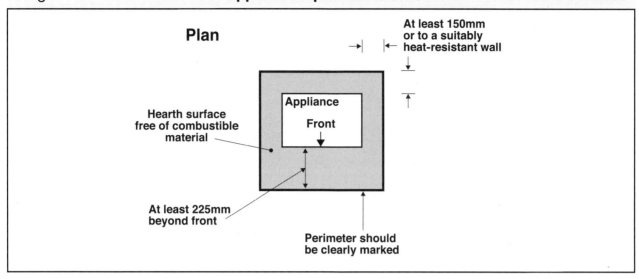

Diagram 39 **Shielding of appliances**

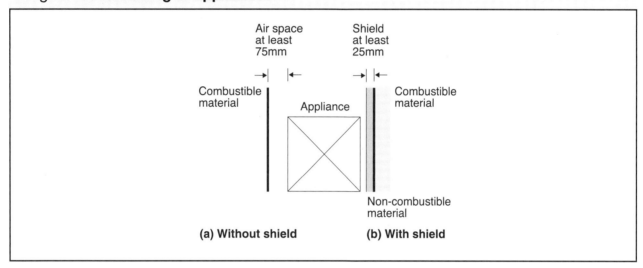

Alternative approach

The requirements may also be met by adopting the relevant recommendations in the publications listed below to achieve an equivalent level of performance to that obtained by following the guidance in this Approved Document:

BS 5440 Installation and maintenance of *flues* and ventilation for gas appliances of rated input not exceeding 70kW net (1st, 2nd and 3rd family gases), Part 1:2008 Specification for installation and maintenance of *flues*; Part 2:2009 Specification for installation and maintenance of ventilation for gas appliances.

BS 5546:2000 Specification for installation of hot water supplies for domestic purposes, using gas-fired appliances of rated input not exceeding 70kW.

BS 5864:2004 Specification for installation in domestic premises of gas-fired ducted-air heaters of rated input not exceeding 60kW.

BS 5871 Specification for installation of gas fires, convector heaters, fire/back boilers and decorative fuel effect gas appliances, Part 1:2005 Gas fires, convector heaters and fire/back boilers and heating stoves (1st, 2nd and 3rd family gases); Part 2:2005 Inset live fuel effect gas fires of heat input not exceeding 15kW and fire/back boilers (2nd and 3rd family gases); Part 3:2005 Decorative fuel effect gas appliances of heat input not exceeding 20kW (2nd and 3rd family gases).

BS 6172:2004 Specification for installation of domestic gas cooking appliances (1st, 2nd and 3rd family gases).

BS 6173:2001 Specification for installation of gas-fired catering appliances for use in all types of catering establishments (2nd and 3rd family gases).

BS 6798:2009 Specification for installation of gas-fired boilers of rated input not exceeding 70kW net.

Section 4: Additional provisions for oil burning appliances with a rated output up to 45kW

Scope

4.1 This guidance is relevant to combustion installations designed to burn oils meeting the specifications for Class C2 (Kerosene) and Class D (Gas oil) given in BS 2869:2006 or equivalent, liquid biofuel conforming to EN 14213:2003 and blends of mineral oil and liquid biofuel.

Appliances fitted in bathrooms and shower rooms

4.2 Open-flued oil-fired appliances should not be installed in rooms such as bathrooms and bedrooms where there is an increased risk of carbon monoxide poisoning. Where locating *combustion appliances* in such rooms cannot be avoided, a way of meeting the requirements would be to provide *room-sealed appliances*.

Air supply to appliances

4.3 A way of meeting the requirements would be to adopt the general guidance given in Section 1, starting at Paragraph 1.2, and to provide permanently open air vents as shown in Diagram 40 in rooms or spaces containing appliances. An example calculation illustrating the use of this guidance is given in Appendix D. Where manufacturers' *installation instructions* require greater areas of permanently open air vents than those shown in Diagram 40, the manufacturers' advice should be followed.

Size of flues (other than balanced flues and flues designed to discharge through or adjacent to walls)

4.4 *Flues* should be sized to suit the intended appliance such that they ensure adequate discharge velocity to prevent flow reversal problems but do not impose excessive flow resistances. A way of meeting the requirements would be to use:

a. connecting *fluepipes* of the same size as the appliance *flue outlet*; and

b. *flues* in *chimneys* of the same cross-sectional area as the appliance *flue outlet*.

When constructing masonry or *flueblock chimneys*, a way of doing this would be to:

i. make the *flue* the same size as the appliance *flue outlet*; or

ii. make the *flue* larger and of a size that would allow the later insertion of a suitable flexible *flue liner* matching the appliance to be installed.

4.5 Larger *flues* may need to be provided where appliance manufacturers' *installation instructions* demand this.

Outlets from flues and flue heights

4.6 The outlet from a *flue* should be so situated externally as to ensure: the correct operation of a *natural draught flue*; the intake of air if a *balanced flue*; and dispersal of the products of combustion.

4.7 A way of meeting the requirement could be to follow the guidance in Diagram 41. The separations given in the Table to Diagram 41 are minimum values that may have to be increased where there is a risk that local factors such as wind patterns could disrupt the operation of the *flue* or where a *natural draught flue* would not be tall enough to clear the products of combustion of an *open-flued appliance*. For *flues* in proximity to roof windows the minimum separation distances identified in Diagram 35 should be applied.

Note: The plume of wet flue products from condensing boilers, positioned in accordance with the safety distances set out in Diagram 41, can sometimes be considered a nuisance for neighbouring properties. Whilst this nuisance is not considered to be within the scope of building regulations, such installations could be considered as a 'Statutory Nuisance' as set out in the Environmental Protection Act. As such, installers may wish to adopt the guidance in Chapter 6 of the *Guide to Condensing Boiler Installation Assessment Procedure for Dwellings.*

Care may also need to be taken to locate *flue outlets* away from parts of the building that may be damaged by frequent wetting.

4.8 *Flue outlets* should be protected with terminal guards if persons could come into contact with them or if they could be damaged. If a *flue outlet* is in a vulnerable position, such as where the *flue* discharges at a point within reach of the ground, balcony, veranda or a window, it should be designed to prevent the entry of any matter that could obstruct the flow.

Diagram 40 Free areas of permanently open air vents for oil-fired appliance installations

	Open flued	Room sealed
Appliance in a room or space	Open flued appliance 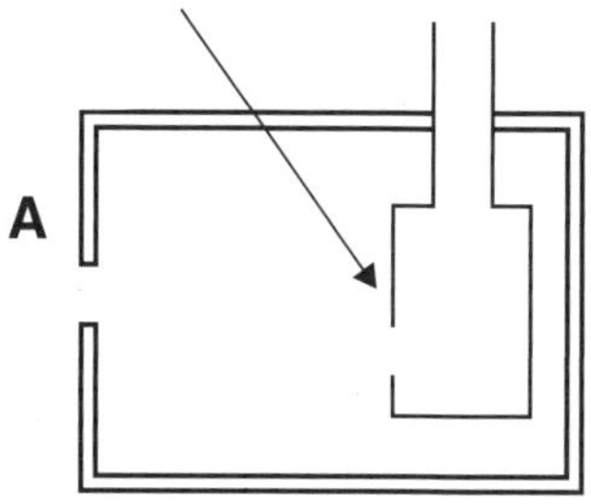 A A = 550mm² per kW output (see Note 3 and 5)	Room-sealed appliance 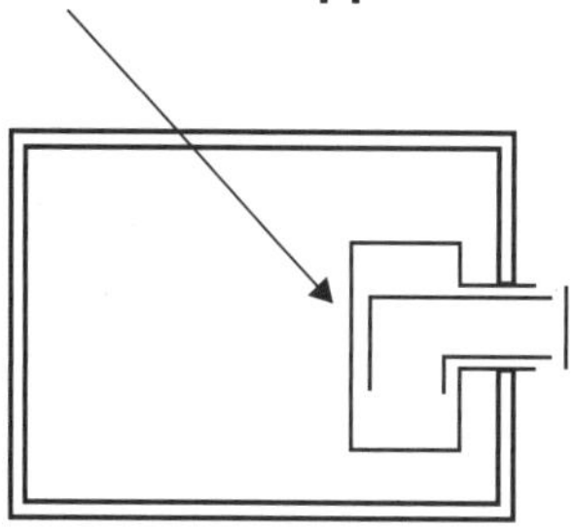 No vent needed
Appliance in an appliance compartment ventilated via an adjoining room or space	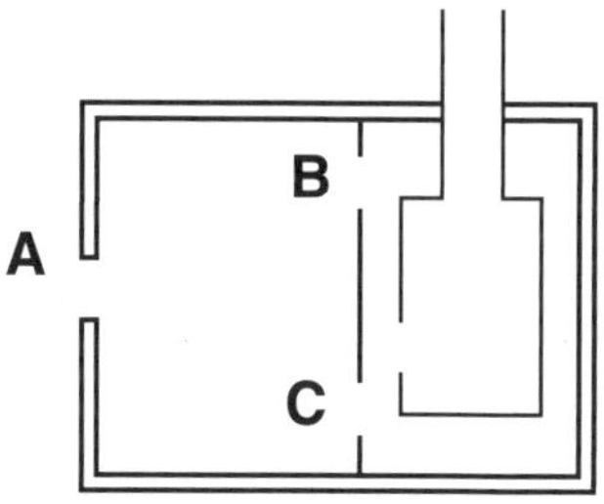 A B C A = 550mm² per kW output (see Note 3 and 5) B = 1100mm² per kW output C = 1650mm² per kW output	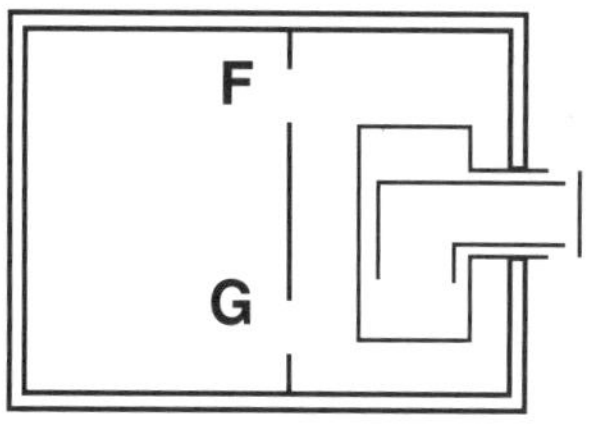 F G F = 1100mm² per kW output G = F
Appliance in an appliance compartment ventilated direct to outside	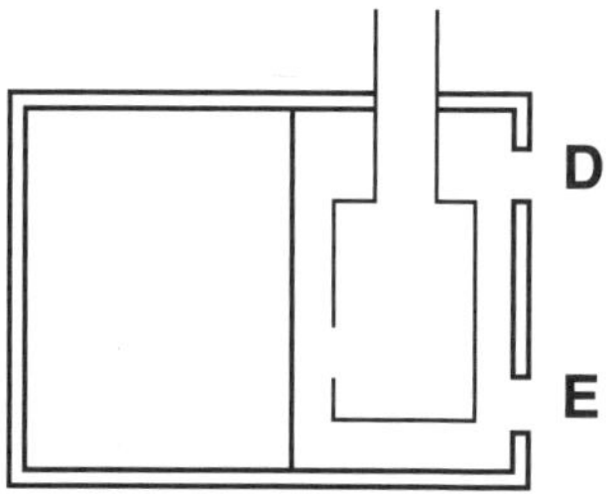 D E D = 550mm² per kW output E = 1100mm² per kW output	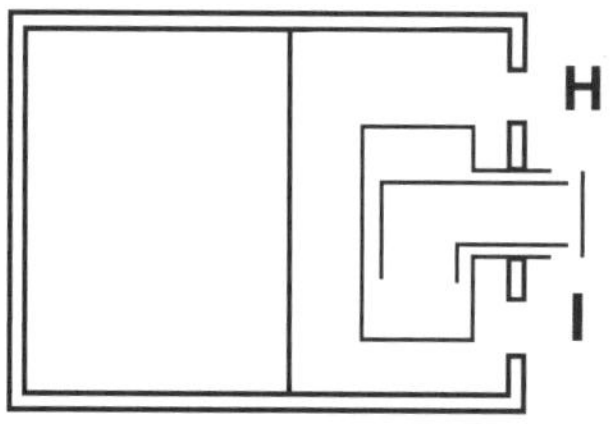 H I H = 550mm² per kW output I = H

Notes:

1. A, D, E, H and I are permanently open vents to the outside. B, C, F and G are permanently open vents between an appliance compartment and a room or space.

2. The area given above is the free area of the vent(s) or the equivalent free area for ventilators of more complex design.

3. Vent A should be increased by a further 550mm² per kW output if the appliance is fitted with a draught break.

4. Divide the area given above in mm² by 100 to find the corresponding area in cm².

5. In older dwellings with an air permeability which is more than 5.0m³/hr/m² the first 5kW(net) can be ignored.

ADDITIONAL PROVISIONS FOR OIL BURNING APPLIANCES WITH A RATED OUTPUT UP TO 45kW

Diagram 41 Location of outlets from flues serving oil-fired appliances

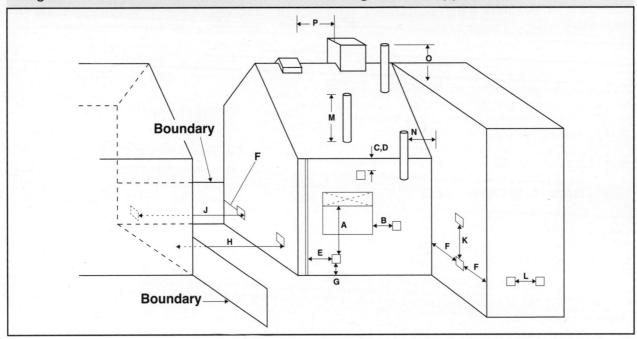

Table to Diagram 41 Location of outlets from flues serving oil-fired appliances

Minimum separation distances for terminals in mm

	Location of outlet (1)	Appliance with pressure jet burner	Appliance with vaporising burner
A	Below an opening (2, 3)	600	Should not be used
B	Horizontally to an opening (2, 3)	600	Should not be used
C	Below a plastic/painted gutter, drainage pipe or eaves if combustible material protected (4)	75	Should not be used
D	Below a balcony or a plastic/painted gutter, drainage pipe or eaves without protection to combustible material	600	Should not be used
E	From vertical sanitary pipework	300	Should not be used
F	From an external or internal corner or from a surface or boundary alongside the terminal	300	Should not be used
G	Above ground or balcony level	300	Should not be used
H	From a surface or boundary facing the terminal	600	Should not be used
J	From a terminal facing the terminal	1200	Should not be used
K	Vertically from a terminal on the same wall	1500	Should not be used
L	Horizontally from a terminal on the same wall	750	Should not be used
M	Above the highest point of an intersection with the roof	600 (6)	1000 (5)
N	From a vertical structure to the side of the terminal	750 (6)	2300
O	Above a vertical structure which is less than 750mm (pressure jet burner) or 2300mm (vaporising burner) horizontally from the side of the terminal	600 (6)	1000 (5)
P	From a ridge terminal to a vertical structure on the roof	1500	Should not be used

Notes:

1. Terminals should only be positioned on walls where appliances have been approved for such configurations when tested in accordance with BS EN 303-1:1999 or OFTEC standards OFS A100 or OFS A101.

2. An opening means an openable element, such as an openable window, or a permanent opening such as a permanently open air vent.

3. Notwithstanding the dimensions above, a terminal should be at least 300mm from combustible material, e.g. a window frame.

4. A way of providing protection of combustible material would be to fit a heat shield at least 750mm wide.

5. Where a terminal is used with a vaporising burner, the terminal should be at least 2300mm horizontally from the roof.

6. Outlets for vertical balanced flues in locations M, N and O should be in accordance with manufacturer's instructions.

Flues for oil-fired appliances: flue gas temperature

4.9 Satisfactory provision of *chimneys* and *fluepipes* depends upon the flue gas temperature to be expected in normal service and separate guidance is given in this Approved Document according to whether the proposed installation will have a flue gas temperature more than or less than 250°C as measured by a suitable method such as those in OFTEC Standards A100 or A101. Suitable *chimney* systems may then be selected based on their performance *designation* having been tested in accordance with the relevant European standard.

4.10 Flue gas temperatures depend upon appliance types and the age of their design. Modern boilers bearing the CE mark, indicating compliance with the *Boiler (Efficiency) Regulations (1993)*, normally have flue gas temperatures not exceeding 250°C. Condensing oil-fired appliances will normally produce flue gas temperatures well below 100°C. Information for individual appliances should be sought from the manufacturer's *installation instructions*, from the manufacturers themselves or from OFTEC. Where this is not available, *flues* should be constructed for an assumed flue gas temperature greater than 250°C.

Provisions for flue gas temperatures in excess of 250°C

4.11 A way of making satisfactory provision for oil appliances in these cases would be to follow the guidance given in Sections 1 and 2 for connecting *fluepipes* and masonry or *flueblock chimneys* or to provide a *factory-made metal* chimney in accordance with Paragraphs 1.42 to 1.46 in Section 1 (but not Paragraph 1.42(b)). However, other products may be acceptable if they have been *certified* for this purpose.

Provisions for flue gas temperatures not exceeding 250°C

4.12 Satisfactory provision of *chimneys* and *fluepipes* for oil appliances in these cases may be achieved by:

a. following the guidance on the selection of components and the manner of their installation as given in Paragraphs 4.13 to 4.20 and the references to Section 1 or (if the intended appliance is new and of known type);

b. i) using factory-made components that achieve a performance at least equal to that corresponding to the *designation* given in Table 8 (for the intended appliance type) when tested to an appropriate European *chimney* standard (BS EN); and

ii) installing these components in accordance with the guidance in Paragraphs 4.13 to 4.20 and Section 1, as relevant, and in accordance with the appliance manufacturer's and component manufacturer's *installation instructions*.

Table 8 Minimum performance designations for chimney and fluepipe components for use with new oil-fired appliances with flue gas temperature less than 250ºC

Appliance type	Minimum designation	Fuel type
Condensing boiler, including combination boiler, range cooker, range cooker/boiler – with pressure-jet burners	T120 N2 W1 O	Class C2 oil (kerosene) Liquid biofuel conforming to EN 14213:2003
Condensing boiler, including combination boiler, range cooker, range cooker/boiler – with pressure-jet burners	T160 N2 W2 O	Class D oil (heating oil)
Non-condensing boiler, including combination boiler, range cooker, range cooker/boiler – with pressure-jet burners	T250 N2 D1 O	Class C2 oil (kerosene) Liquid biofuel conforming to EN 14213:2003
Non-condensing boiler, including combination boiler, range cooker, range cooker/boiler – with pressure-jet burners	T250 N2 D2 O	Class D oil (heating oil)
Cooker and room heater – with vaporising burner	T160 N2 D1 O	Class C2 oil (kerosene)
Cooker and room heater – with vaporising burner	T250 N2 D2 O	Class D oil (heating oil)

Notes:

1. The designation of chimney products is described in Appendix G. The BS EN for the product will specify its full designation and marking requirements.

2. These are default designations. Where the appliance manufacturer's installation instructions specify a higher designation, this should be complied with.

3. Refer to the appliance manufacturer regarding the suitability of the appliance and flue system for use with oil / bio-liquid blends.

Connecting fluepipe components

4.13 Connecting *fluepipes* can be constructed using the following components:

a. any of the options listed in Paragraph 1.32; or

b. sheet metal *fluepipes* as described in BS EN 1856-2:2004; or

c. fibre cement pipes as described in BS EN 1857:2003+A1:2008; or

d. any other component that has been certified as suitable for this purpose.

Masonry chimneys

4.14   Masonry *chimneys* can be built in accordance with Paragraphs 1.27 and 1.28 in Section 1.

Flueblock chimneys

4.15   *Chimneys* can be constructed from factory-made flueblock systems primarily designed for solid fuel, as described in Paragraphs 1.29 and 1.30 in Section 1. They can also be constructed from factory-made flueblock systems comprising straight blocks, recess units, lintel blocks, offset blocks, transfer blocks and jointing materials complying with:

a.   BS EN 1858:2003 for concrete flueblocks; or

b.   BS EN 1806:2006 for clay/ceramic flueblocks, with a performance at least equal to the *designation* given in Table 8 for the intended appliance type.

4.16   *Flueblock chimneys* should be installed with sealed joints in accordance with the flueblock manufacturer's *installation instructions*. Where bends or offsets are required, these should be formed using matching factory-made components. Flueblocks which are not intended to be bonded into surrounding masonry should be supported and restrained in accordance with the manufacturer's *installation instructions*.

Factory-made metal chimneys

4.17   *Chimneys* for oil-fired appliances can be constructed using the systems described in Paragraphs 1.42 to 1.46 in Section 1.

Location and shielding of flues

4.18   A way of protecting the building fabric from the heat dissipation from *flues*, where flue gas temperatures are not expected to exceed 250°C, would be to follow the guidance in Table 9.

4.19   Where a *fluepipe* or *chimney* penetrates a *fire compartment* wall or floor, it must not breach the fire separation requirements of Part B. See Approved Document B for more guidance.

4.20   *Fluepipes* and factory-made *chimneys* should also be guarded if they could be at risk of damage or if they present a hazard to people that is not immediately apparent such as when they traverse intermediate floors out of sight of the appliance.

Table 9 Protecting buildings from hot flues for flue gas temperatures not more than 250°C

Flue within:	Protection measures
Connecting fluepipe Factory-made chimney designated in accordance with BS EN 1856-1:2003	Flues should be at least 25mm from any combustible material (measured from the outer surface of the flue wall, or the outer surface of the inner wall in the case of multi-walled products). Where passing through a combustible wall, floor or roof (other than a compartment wall floor or roof) this separation can be achieved by a non-combustible sleeve enclosing the fluepipe or chimney with a 25mm air-space to the relevant flue wall. (The air-space could be wholly or partially filled with non-combustible insulating material.)
Factory-made chimney designated in accordance with BS EN 1856-1:2003 and BS EN 1856-2:2004	Install in accordance with Paragraph 1.45 of this Approved Document with minimum separation distances according to flue designation.
Masonry chimney	Provide at least 25mm of masonry between flues and any combustible material.
Flueblock chimney	Provide flueblock walls at least 25mm thick.
Flue assemblies for room-sealed appliances	a) flues passing through combustible walls should be surrounded by insulating material at least 50mm thick. b) provide a clearance of at least 50mm from the edge of the flue outlet to any combustible wall cladding.

Relining of flues in chimneys

4.21   Lining or relining *flues* may be building work and, in any case, such work should be carried out so that the objectives of requirements J2 to J4 are met (see Paragraphs 1.34 and 1.35). For *flue liners* serving oil appliances, ways of meeting the requirements include the use of:

a.   linings suitable for use if the flue gas temperature can be expected to exceed 250°C such as:

  i.   liners as described in Paragraph 1.27;

  ii.   liners as described in Paragraph 2.20;

  iii.   flexible stainless steel liners designated in accordance with BS EN 1858:2008;

  iv.   other systems which have been certified as suitable for this purpose.

b. linings suitable for use if the flue gas temperature is unlikely to exceed 250°C such as:

   i. any of the linings described in (a) above;

   ii. other systems which have been certified as suitable for this purpose;

   iii. (if the appliance is new and of known type) flue lining systems that have a performance at least equal to that corresponding to the *designation* given in Table 8 for the intended appliance type.

4.22   Flexible metal *flue liners* should be installed in one complete length without joints within the *chimney*. Other than for sealing at the top and the bottom, the space between the *chimney* and the liner should be left empty unless this is contrary to the manufacturer's instructions. Double-skin flexible *flue liners* should be installed in accordance with the manufacturer's *installation instructions*. Liners should be installed in accordance with BS EN 15827-1:2007.

Flues for appliances burning Class D oil

4.23   *Flues* which may be expected to serve appliances burning Class D oil should be made of materials which are resistant to acids of sulphur, i.e. minimum flue *designation* 'D2' for non-condensing appliances or 'W2' for condensing appliances, according to the *designation* system in BS EN 1443:2003 and related flue standards.

Hearths for oil-fired appliances

4.24   *Hearths* are needed to prevent the building catching fire and, whilst it is not a health and safety provision, it is customary to top them with a tray for collecting spilled fuel.

4.25   If the operation of an appliance is unlikely to cause the temperature of the floor below it to exceed 100°C, as shown using an appropriate test procedure such as those in *OFTEC Standards A 100 and A 101*, special measures may be unnecessary beyond the provision of a rigid, imperforate, and non-absorbent sheet of *non-combustible material* such as a steel tray. This may be provided as an integral part of the appliance.

4.26   If the appliance could cause the temperature of the floor below it to exceed 100°C, a more substantial *hearth* is required. A way of meeting the requirement would be to provide a *hearth* of solid *non-combustible material* at least 125mm thick (which may include the thickness of any non-combustible floor) with plan dimensions not less than those shown in Diagram 24 in Section 2. It should have no combustible material below it unless there is an air-space of at least 50mm between the material and the underside of the *hearth*, or there is a distance of at least 250mm between the material and the top of the *hearth* (see Diagram 25 in Section 2).

4.27   To provide a region around the appliance which is free of any combustible material, the appliance should not be placed closer to the edges of the *hearth* nor closer to any combustible material which is laid over the *hearth* than the distances shown in Diagram 42. The perimeter of this safe region should be marked to provide a warning to the building occupants and to discourage combustible floor finishes such as carpet from being laid too close to the appliance. A way of achieving this would be to provide a change in level.

Shielding of oil-fired appliances

4.28   Combustible materials adjacent to oil-fired appliances may need protection from the effects of heat. Special measures may be unnecessary if the materials will not be subjected to temperatures in excess of 100°C, but otherwise a way of meeting the requirement would be to protect combustible fabric with:

a. a shield of *non-combustible material*, such as insulating board with fire-resistant surface; or

b. an air-space of at least 75mm (see Diagram 39 in Section 3).

4.29   Appliances having surface temperatures during normal operation of no more than 100°C would not normally require shielding.

Alternative approach

The requirements may also be met by adopting the relevant recommendations in the publication listed below to achieve an equivalent level of performance to that obtained by following the guidance in this Approved Document: BS 5410-1:1997 *Code of practice for oil firing. Installations up to 45kW output capacity for space heating and hot water supply purposes*.

Diagram 42 **Location of an oil-fired appliance in relation to its hearth. Minimum dimensions of the heat-resistant material in the hearth and the clear zone of non-combustible surface**

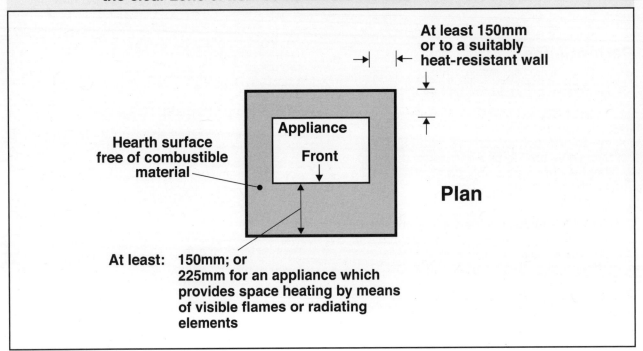

Section 5: Provisions for liquid fuel storage and supply

Performance

5.1   In the Secretary of State's view requirements J5 and J6 will be met if:

a. oil and LPG fuel storage installations including the pipework connecting them to the *combustion appliances* in the buildings they serve are located and constructed so that they are reasonably protected from fires which may occur in buildings or beyond *boundaries*;

b. oil storage tanks, their ancillary equipment and the pipework connecting them to *combustion appliances* in buildings used wholly or mainly for private dwellings:

   i. are reasonably resistant to physical damage and corrosion and are designed and installed so as to minimise the risk of oil escaping during the filling or maintenance of the tank; and

   ii. incorporate secondary containment when there is a significant risk of pollution; and

   iii. are labelled with information on how to respond to a leak.

Heating oil storage installations

5.2   Guidance is given in this Approved Document on ways of meeting requirements J5 and J6 when proposing to construct oil storage systems with above-ground or semi-buried tanks of 3500 litres *capacity* or less, used exclusively for heating oil. Heating oils comprise Class C2 oil (kerosene) or Class D oil (gas oil) as specified in BS 2869:1998, liquid biofuel conforming to EN 14213:2003 and blends of mineral oil and liquid biofuel. A way of meeting requirements J5 and J6 for such installations would be to follow the relevant recommendations in BS 5410-1:1997, whilst also adopting the guidance in paragraphs 5.4 to 5.12.

5.3   Requirement J6 does not apply to oil storage systems where the *capacity* of the tank exceeds 3500 litres, or where the tank is fully buried or where the building served is not wholly or mainly used as one or more private dwellings. However, requirement J5 applies to oil storage systems serving buildings of all descriptions, where the capacity of the tank exceeds 90 litres, with no upper *capacity* limit on application, and including cases where the tank is buried. For tanks with capacities in excess of 3500 litres, advice on ways of complying with requirements J5 and any other fire precautions legislation may be sought from the Fire Authority. In England tanks serving buildings which are not wholly or

mainly used as private dwellings are likely to be subject to the Control of Pollution (Oil Storage) (England) Regulations 2001 (see paragraph 5.7).

Protective measures against fire

5.4   A way of achieving compliance with requirement J5 would be to adopt the guidance given in Table 10, which also offers advice on reducing the risk of fuel storage system fires igniting buildings and to make provision against the installation becoming overgrown. This can be achieved with a hard surface beneath the tank such as concrete, or paving slabs at least 42mm thick, extending out at least 300mm beyond the perimeter of the tank (or its external skin if it is of the integrally bunded type).

Table 10 **Fire protection for oil storage tanks**

Location of tank	Protection usually satisfactory
Within a building	Locate tanks in a place of special fire hazard which should be directly ventilated to outside. Without prejudice to the need for compliance with all the requirements in Schedule 1, the need to comply with Part B should particularly be taken into account.
Less than 1800mm from any part of a building	a) Make building walls imperforate (1) within 1800mm of tanks with at least 30 minutes fire resistance (2) to internal fire and construct eaves. b) Provide a fire wall (3) between the tank and any part of the building within 1800mm of the tank and construct eaves as in (a) above. The fire wall should extend at least 300mm higher and wider than the affected parts of the tank.
Less than 760mm from a boundary	Provide a fire wall between the tank and the boundary or a boundary wall having at least 30 minutes fire resistance to fire on either side. The fire wall or the boundary wall should extend at least 300mm higher and wider than the top and sides of the tank.
At least 1800mm from the building and at least 760mm from a boundary	No further provisions necessary.

Notes:

1. Excluding small openings such as air bricks etc.

2. Fire resistance in terms of insulation, integrity and stability as determined by testing to the relevant parts of BS 476 or BS EN 1363 or BS EN 1364.

3. Fire walls are imperforate non-combustible walls or screens, such as masonry walls or fire-rated composite panel screens.

5.5 *Fire walls* should be built to be stable so as not to pose a danger to people around them. A way of achieving this when constructing masonry walls would be to follow the guidance on wall thickness in relation to height given in *Your garden walls: Better to be safe than sorry* (See 'Other Publications referred to').

Oil supply pipe systems: means of automatic isolation

5.6 A way of meeting the requirement would be to install fuel pipework which is resistant to the effects of fire and to fit a proprietary fire valve system in accordance with the relevant recommendations in BS 5410-1:1997, Sections 8.2 and 8.3.

Provisions where there is a risk of oil pollution

5.7 The Control of Pollution (Oil Storage) (England) Regulations 2001 (SI 2001/2954) came into force on 1 March 2002. They apply to a wide range of oil storage installations in England, but they do not apply to the storage of oil on any premises used wholly or mainly as one or more private dwellings, if the *capacity* of the tank is 3500 litres or less. Advice on the construction of above-ground oil storage tanks that may be subject to these Regulations is contained in *Above Ground Oil Storage Tanks: PPG2 (2004)*.

Note: Below ground oil storage is not recommended where other options are available as underground tanks are difficult to inspect and leaks may not be immediately obvious. Some guidance and further sources of reference are contained in *installation, decommissioning and removal of underground storage tanks: PPG27(2002)*.

5.8 Requirement J6 applies to oil storage tanks of 3500 litres or less serving *combustion appliances* in buildings used wholly or mainly as private dwellings. In such cases, secondary containment should be provided where there is a significant risk of oil pollution. For the purposes of requirement J6, there is a significant risk of pollution if the oil storage installation:

a. has a total *capacity* of more than 2500 litres; or

b. is located within 10m of inland freshwaters or coastal waters; or

c. is located where spillage could run into an open drain or to a loose-fitting manhole cover; or

d. is located within 50m of sources of potable water, such as wells, bore-holes or springs; or

e. is located where oil spilled from the installation could reach the waters listed above by running across hard ground; or

f. is located where tank vent pipe outlets cannot be seen from the intended filling point.

g. is located within Zone 1 (inner protection zone) of an Environment Agency Groundwater Source Protection Zone (SPZ).

Note: The location of SPZs is shown on the Environment Agency's Groundwater Sources map available online at www.environment-agency.gov.uk/research/library/maps.

5.9 Inland freshwaters include streams, rivers, reservoirs and lakes, as well as ditches and ground drainage (including perforated drainage pipes) that feed into them.

5.10 When secondary containment is considered necessary, a way of meeting the requirement would be to:

a. provide an integrally bunded prefabricated tank; or

b. construct a bund from masonry or concrete in accordance with the general guidance in Above Ground Oil Storage Tanks: PPG2 (2004) and the specific advice in Masonry Bunds for Oil Storage Tanks or Concrete Bunds for Oil Storage Tanks, as appropriate. However:

c. where the bund walls are part of the walls of a chamber or building enclosing the tank, any door through such walls should be above bund level; and

d. specialist advice should be sought where the bund has a structural role as part of a building.

5.11 Bunds, whether part of prefabricated tank systems or constructed on site, should have a *capacity* of at least 110 per cent of the largest tank they contain. Integrally bunded oil tanks that comply with the following standards will meet this provision:

   i. OFS T100 Oil Firing Equipment Standard – Polyethylene Oil Storage Tanks for Distillate Fuels (2008);

  ii. OFS T100 Oil Firing Equipment Standard – Steel Oil Storage Tanks and Tank Bunds for use with Distillate Fuels, Lubrication Oils and Waste Oils (2008).

5.12 An oil storage installation should carry a label in a prominent position giving advice on what to do if an oil spill occurs and the telephone number of the Environment Agency's Emergency Hotline (see Appendix F).

LPG storage installations

5.13 LPG installations are controlled by legislation enforced by the HSE or their agents. Factors which determine the amount of building work necessary for a LPG storage installation to comply include its *capacity*, whether tanks are installed above or below ground and the nature of the premises they serve. A storage installation may be shown to comply with the legislation by constructing it in accordance with an appropriate industry Code of Practice, prepared in consultation with the HSE. However, for an installation of up to 1.1 tonne *capacity*, whose tank stands in the open air, following the guidance in this Approved Document and the relevant guidance in Approved Document B, will normally ensure that no further building work is needed to comply with other legislation.

Tank location and protective measures

5.14 For LPG storage systems of up to 1.1 tonne *capacity*, comprising one tank standing in the open air, a way of meeting the requirement J5 would be to comply with the relevant recommendations in the UKLPG *Code Of Practice 1: Bulk LPG Storage at Fixed Installations Part 1 (2009)* and BS 5482-1:2005 (see Appendix F and 'Other Publications referred to') whilst also adopting the following guidance:

5.15 The LPG tank should be installed outdoors and not within an open pit. The tank should be adequately separated from buildings, the *boundary* and any fixed sources of ignition to enable safe dispersal in the event of venting or leaks and in the event of fire to reduce the risk of fire spreading. A way of meeting the requirements in normal situations would be to adopt the separation distances in Table 11 and Diagram 43, which also offers advice on reducing the risk of LPG storage fires igniting the building. Drains, gullies and cellar hatches within the separation distances should be protected from gas entry.

5.16 *Fire walls* may be free-standing walls built between the tank and the building, *boundary* and fixed source of ignition (see Diagram 43 (b)) or a part of the building or a boundary wall belonging to the property. Where a *fire wall* is part of the building or a boundary wall, it should be located in accordance with Diagram 43(c) and, if part of the building, constructed in accordance with Diagram 43(d).

5.17 Suitable *fire walls* would be imperforate and of solid masonry, concrete or similar construction. They should have a *fire resistance* (insulation, integrity and stability (REI)) of at least 30 minutes but, if part of the building as shown in Diagram 43 (d), they should have a *fire resistance* (REI) of at least 60 minutes. To ensure good ventilation, *fire walls* should not normally be built on more than one side of a tank.

5.18 A *fire wall* should be at least as high as the pressure relief valve. It should extend horizontally such that the separation specified in Table 11 (Column B) is maintained:

a. when measured around the ends of the *fire wall* as shown in Diagram 43(b); or

b. when measured to the ends of the *fire wall* as shown in Diagram 43(c), if the *fire wall* is the *boundary* or part of the building.

Location and support of cylinders

5.19 Where an LPG storage installation consists of a set of cylinders, a way of meeting the requirements would be to follow the provisions below and as shown in Diagram 44.

5.20 Provisions should enable cylinders to stand upright, secured by straps or chains against a wall outside the building in a well-ventilated position at ground level, where they are readily accessible, reasonably protected from physical damage and where they do not obstruct exit routes from the building. Satisfactory building work provisions would be to provide a firm level base such as concrete at least 50mm thick or paving slabs bedded on mortar at a location so that cylinder valves will be:

a. at least 1m horizontally and 300mm vertically from openings in the building or heat sources such as flue terminals and tumble-dryer vents; and

b. at least 2m horizontally from drains without traps, unsealed gullies or cellar hatches unless an intervening wall not less than 250mm high is provided.

Table 11 Fire protection for LPG storage tanks (see Diagram 43)

(A) Capacity of tank not exceeding (tonnes):	Minimum separation distances from buildings, boundaries or fixed sources of ignition (metres)	
	(B) To a tank with no fire wall or to a tank around a fire wall	(C) To a tank shielded by a fire wall
0.25	2.5	0.3
1.1	3	1.5

Combustion appliances and fuel storage systems

Diagram 43   Separation or shielding of liquefied petroleum gas tanks of up to 1.1 tonne capacity from buildings, boundaries and fixed sources of ignition

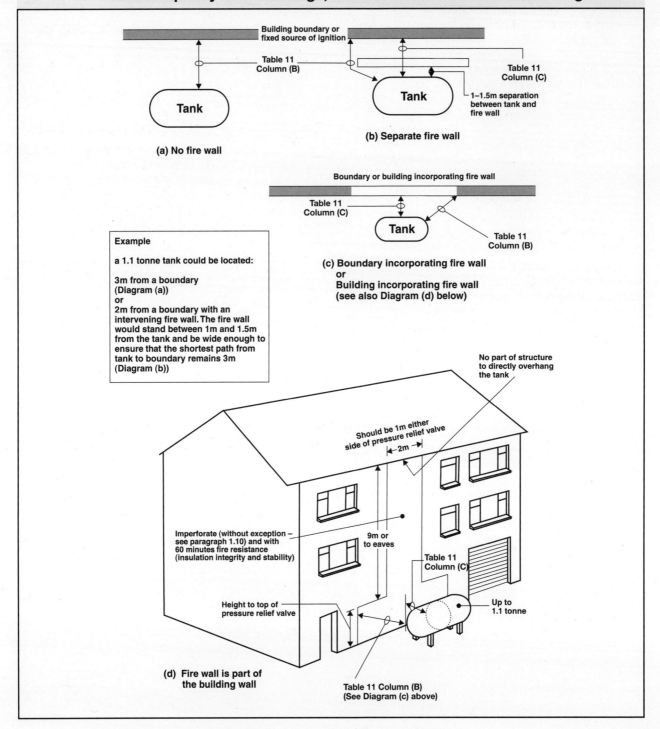

Building boundary or fixed source of ignition

Table 11 Column (B)

Tank

(a) No fire wall

Table 11 Column (C)

1–1.5m separation between tank and fire wall

Tank

(b) Separate fire wall

Boundary or building incorporating fire wall

Table 11 Column (C)

Table 11 Column (B)

Tank

(c) Boundary incorporating fire wall
or
**Building incorporating fire wall
(see also Diagram (d) below)**

Example

a 1.1 tonne tank could be located:

3m from a boundary
(Diagram (a))
or
2m from a boundary with an intervening fire wall. The fire wall would stand between 1m and 1.5m from the tank and be wide enough to ensure that the shortest path from tank to boundary remains 3m (Diagram (b))

No part of structure to directly overhang the tank

Should be 1m either side of pressure relief valve

|←2m→|

Imperforate (without exception – see paragraph 1.10) and with 60 minutes fire resistance (insulation integrity and stability)

9m or to eaves

Table 11 Column (C)

Up to 1.1 tonne

Height to top of pressure relief valve

Table 11 Column (B)
(See Diagram (c) above)

(d) Fire wall is part of the building wall

Diagram 44 **Location of LPG cylinders**

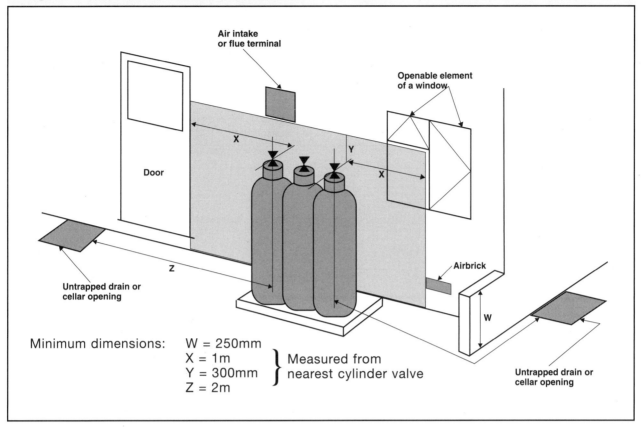

Air intake
or flue terminal

Openable element
of a window

Door

X

Y

X

Untrapped drain or
cellar opening

Z

Airbrick

W

Untrapped drain or
cellar opening

Minimum dimensions: W = 250mm
X = 1m
Y = 300mm } Measured from
nearest cylinder valve
Z = 2m

LPG pipework (Informative)

5.21   For the puposes of the Gas Safety
(Installation and Use) Regulations 1998 (GSIUR),
where the LPG service pipework runs underground
from the LPG tank to the premises it should be
manufactured of non-corroding material. Pipe
entering the building should be manufactured
from metallic material and the transition joints
between the non-metallic and metallic pipe
should be located outdoors. The pipe should
enter the building above ground and be sleeved.
The sleeve should be continuous through the
external wall and be sealed at the inner wall to
ensure that any escapes of gas are vented to the
outside only. Further guidance is available in
UKLPG Code of Practice 22 and Institution of
Gas Engineers and Managers standard IG/TD/4.

5.22   In respect of installation pipework subject
to the provisions of the GSIUR, Regulation 19(6)
of the GSIUR requires that installation pipework
should not be installed in any shaft, duct or void
which is not adequately ventilated. This is also
applicable to LPG pipework in buildings not
subject to GSIUR. Guidance on the ventilation
of pipe in ducts can be found in BS 8131:1997
Code of Practice for accommodation of building
services in ducts.

Appendix A: Checklist for checking and testing of hearths, fireplaces, flues and chimneys

EXAMPLES: SEE PARAGRAPH 1.55

Hearth, fireplace, flues and chimneys

The checklist can help you to ensure hearths, fireplaces, flues and chimneys are satisfactory. If you have been directly engaged, copies should also be offered to the client and to the Building Control Body to show what you have done to comply with the requirements of Part J. If you are a sub-contractor, a copy should be offered to the main contractor.

1.	Building address, where work has been carried out			

2.	Identification of hearth, fireplace, chimney or flue.	*Example:* *Fireplace in lounge*	*Example:* *Gas fire in rear addition bedroom*	*Example:* *Small boiler room*
3.	Firing capability: solid fuel/gas/oil/all.	*All*	*Gas only*	*Oil only*
4.	Intended type of appliance. State type or make. If open fire give finished fireplace opening dimensions.	*Open fire* *480 W x 560 H (mm)*	*Radiant/convector fire 6kW input*	*Oil fire boiler 18kW output (pressure jet)*
5.	Ventilation provisions for the appliance: State type and area of permanently open air vents.	*2 through wall ventilators each 10,000mm² (100cm²)*	*Not fitted*	*Vents to outside:* *Top 9,900mm²* *Bottom 19,800mm²*
6.	Chimney or flue construction			
a)	State the type and make and whether new or existing.	*New. Brick with clay liners*	*Existing masonry*	*S.S. prefab to BS 4543-2*
b)	Internal flue size (and equivalent height, where calculated – natural draught gas appliances only).	*200mm Ø*	*125mm Ø (H_0=3.3m)*	*127mm Ø*
c)	If clay or concrete flue liners used confirm they are correctly jointed with socket end uppermost and state joining materials used.	*Sockets uppermost Jointed by fire cement*	*Not applicable*	*Not applicable*
d)	If an existing chimney has been refurbished with a new liner, type or make of liner fitted.	*Not applicable to BS 715*	*Flexible metal liner*	*Not applicable*
e)	Details of flue outlet terminal and diagram reference.			
	Outlet detail:	*Smith Ltd Louvred pot 200mm Ø*	*125mm Ø GC1 terminal*	*Maker's recommended terminal*
	Compiles with:	*As Diagram 17, AD J*	*As BS 5440-1:2008*	*As Diagram 41, AD J*
f)	Number and angle of bends.	*2 x 45°*	*2 x 45°*	*1 x 90° Tee*
g)	Provision for cleaning and recommended frequency.	*Sweep annually via fireplace opening*	*Annual service by Gas Safe Register engineer*	*Sweep annually via base of Tee and via appliance*
7.	Hearth, form of construction. New or existing?	*New. Tiles on concrete floor. 125mm thick. As Diagram 25 AD J*	*Existing hearth for solid fuel fire, with fender.*	*New. Solid floor Min 125mm concrete above DPM. As Diagram 42, ADJ*
8.	Inspection and testing after completion Test carried out by: Test (Appendix E in AD J) and results	*Inspected and tested by J Smith, Smith Building Co.*	*Tested by J Smith, GasSafe Reg no. 1234*	*Tested by J Smith, The Oil Heating Co.*
Flue inspection	visual	*Not possible, bends*	*Not possible, bends*	*Checked to Section 10, BS7566:Part 3: 1992 – OK*
	sweeping	*OK*	*Not applicable*	*OK*
	coring ball	*OK*	*Not applicable*	*OK*
	smoke	*OK*	*Not applicable*	*OK*
Appliance (where included)	spillage	*Not included*	*OK*	*OK*

I/We the undersigned confirm that the above details are correct. In my opinion, these works comply with the relevant requirements in Part J of Schedule 1 to the Building Regulations.

Print name and title .... Profession ....

Capacity ...(e.g. "Proprietor of Smith's Flues", Authorising Engineer for Brown plc)... Tel no. ....

Address .... Postcode ....

Signed .... Date ....

Registered membership of ... (e.g. GasSafe, OFTEC, HETAS, NACE, NACS) ....

Blank form – This page may be copied to provide certificates for use

Hearth, fireplace, flues and chimneys

The checklist can help you to ensure that hearths, fireplaces, flues and chimneys are satisfactory. If you have been directly engaged, copies should also be offered to the client and to the Building Control Body to show what you have done to comply with the requirements of Part J. If you are a sub-contractor, a copy should be offered to the main contractor.

1. **Building address, where work has been carried out**...
....
....

2. **Identification of hearth, fireplace, chimney or flue.**

3. **Firing capability: solid fuel/gas/oil/all.**

4. **Intended type of appliance.**
    State type or make. If open fire give finished
    fireplace opening dimensions.

5. **Ventilation provisions for the appliance:**
    State type and area of permanently open air vents.

6. **Chimney or flue construction**

a) **State the type and make and whether new or existing.**

b) **Internal flue size (and equivalent height, where**
    calculated – natural draught gas appliances only).

c) **If clay or concrete flue liners used confirm they are**
    correctly jointed with socket end uppermost and state
    joining materials used.

d) **If an existing chimney has been refurbished with a new**
    liner, type or make of liner fitted.

e) **Details of flue outlet terminal and diagram reference.**

    Outlet detail:

    Complies with:

f) **Number and angle of bends.**

g) **Provision for cleaning and recommended frequency.**

7. **Hearth, form of construction. New or existing?**

8. **Inspection and testing after completion**
    Test carried out by:
    Test (Appendix E in AD J) and results
    Flue inspection   **visual**
    sweeping
    coring ball
    smoke
    Appliance (where included) spillage

I/We the undersigned confirm that the above details are correct. In my opinion, these works comply with the relevant requirements in Part J of Schedule 1 to the Building Regulations.

Print name and title .... Profession ....

Capacity ...(e.g. "Proprietor of Smith's Flues", Authorising Engineer for Brown plc).. Tel no. ....

Address .... Postcode ....

Signed .... Date ....

Registered membership of ... (e.g. GasSafe, OFTEC, HETAS, NACE, NACS) ....

Appendix B: Opening areas of large or unusual fireplaces

(SEE PARAGRAPH 2.7)

B1 The opening area of a fireplace should be calculated from the following formula:

$$\text{Fireplace opening area (mm}^2) = \left(\begin{array}{c} \text{Total horizontal length} \\ \text{of fireplace opening} \\ \text{L (mm)} \end{array} \right) \times \left(\begin{array}{c} \text{Height of fireplace} \\ \text{opening} \\ \text{H (mm)} \end{array} \right)$$

B2 Examples of L and H for large and unusual fireplace openings are shown in Diagram 45.

Diagram 45 Large or unusual fireplace openings. (Note: for use with this Appendix, measure L, H and W in mm)

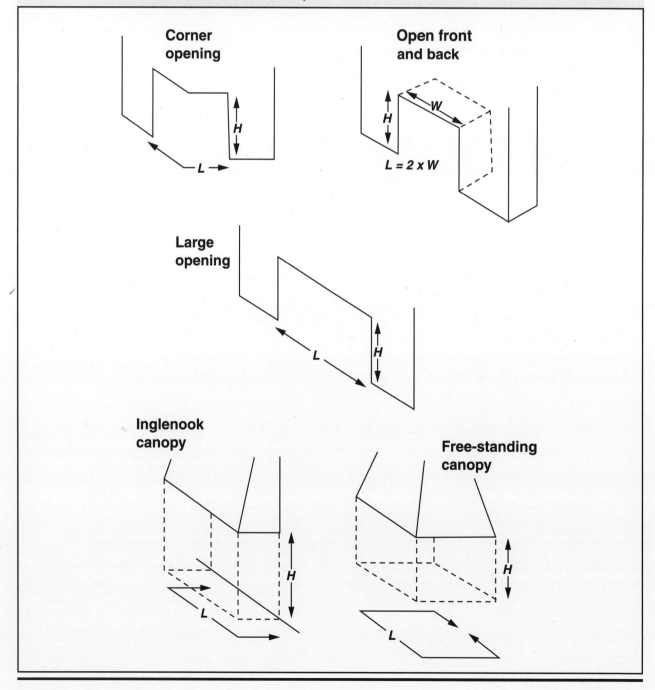

Appendix C: Example calculation of the ventilation requirements of a gas-fired appliance

C1 An open-flued boiler with a rated input of 15kW (net) is installed in an *appliance compartment* such as a boiler room, which is ventilated directly to the outside. The design of the boiler is such that it requires cooling air in these circumstances.

C2 The cooling air is exhausted via vent D, which has an area:

$$15\text{kW} \times 500 \; \frac{\text{mm}^2}{\text{kW}} = 7500\text{mm}^2$$

C3 Vent E allows the cooling air to enter, as well as admitting the air needed for combustion and the safe operation of the *flue*. It has an area:

$$15\text{kW} \times 1000 \; \frac{\text{mm}^2}{\text{kW}} = 15{,}000\text{mm}^2$$

C4 The ventilation areas in cm² can be found by dividing the results given above in mm² by 100.

Appendix D: Example calculation of the ventilation requirements of an oil-fired appliance

D1   An *open-flued appliance* is installed in an *appliance compartment* such as a cupboard, which is ventilated via an adjoining room. The air permeability of the dwelling is 6.0 m³/(h.m²) at 50Pa. The appliance has a rated output of 11kW, i.e. 6kW more than the rating at which permanent ventilation openings become necessary for the adjoining room.

D2   Air for combustion and the safe operation of the *flue* enters the adjoining room partially through infiltration, with the balance entering via vent A, whose area is calculated as follows:

$$(11kW - 5kW) \times 550 \; \frac{mm^2}{kW} = 3300mm^2$$

D3   The cooling air for the *appliance compartment* is exhausted through vent B, which has an area:

$$11kW \times 1100 \; \frac{mm^2}{kW} = 12,100mm^2$$

D4   All of the air for combustion and the safe operation of the *flue* as well as cooling air enters the *appliance compartment* through vent C, which has an area:

$$11kW \times 1650 \; \frac{mm^2}{kW} = 18,150mm^2$$

D5   The ventilation areas in cm² can be found by dividing the results given above in mm² by 100.

Appendix E: Methods of checking compliance with requirement J2

(SEE PARAGRAPHS 1.36 AND 1.54)

E1   This Appendix describes ways of checking the compliance with J2 of existing, relined or new *flues*, and (where included in the work) the *combustion appliance*. It applies only to *natural draught flues* intended for *open-flued appliances*. The procedures described are used only to assess whether the *flue* in the *chimney*, the connecting *fluepipe* (and flue gas passages in the appliance) are free of obstruction and acceptably gas-tight. In addition, appliance performance tests, including flue spillage tests to check for compliance with J2, should be carried out when an appliance is commissioned to check for compliance with Part L and as required by the Gas Safety (Installation and Use) Regulations.

E2   Tests on *flues* should be carried out at the most appropriate time during the building work. Where possible, for example, smoke tests should be performed when the structure of a *chimney* is visible and before the application of finishes such as plaster or dry lining that could obscure sight of smoke leakage during testing.

Testing applications

Tests for existing flues

E3   *Flues* in existing *chimneys* can be obstructed by nests, debris resulting from deterioration of the structure (e.g. brickwork, flue lining material or pieces of *chimney* pot) and by soot and tar. *Flues* in existing *chimneys* may also leak as a result of holes or cracks appearing in the structure and linings, particularly at joints. The top, exposed part of a *chimney* is particularly prone to decay. A way of checking the state of a *flue* prior to bringing it back into use would be to do the following:

a. Sweep the *flue*. This is intended to clean the *flue* to demonstrate that it is essentially free from obstructions and to enable better visual inspection and testing of the *flue*. Tar deposits caused by burning wood may be especially hard to dislodge and should be removed. The debris that comes down the *chimney* when sweeping should be examined for excessive quantities of lining or brick that are signs that further repairs are necessary.

b. Carry out a visual inspection of the accessible parts to identify:

  i.   Deterioration in the structure, connections or linings which could affect the flue's gas-tightness and safe performance with the proposed *combustion appliance*. Examine the interior of the *flue* and the exterior of the *chimney* including in the roof-space. The presence of smoke or tar stains on the exterior of a chimney/breast is a sign of leaks that possibly indicate damage;

  ii. Modifications made whilst the *flue* was out of service, such as the fitting of a ventilator terminal, which would be incompatible with using the *flue* with the intended appliance;

  iii. Correct lining and lining sizes for the proposed new application.

c. Perform checks where necessary to demonstrate that the *flue* is free from restriction: a visual check may be sufficient where the full length of the *flue* can be seen. In cases of doubt, a way of checking this would be to carry out a coring ball test.

d. Check the gas-tightness of the *flue* by carrying out a smoke test.

New masonry and flueblock chimneys

E4   Check during construction that liners are installed the right way up, with sockets facing upwards and joints are sealed so that moisture and condensate will be contained in the *chimney*.

E5   *Flues* in new masonry *chimneys* can be obstructed, particularly at bends, by debris left during construction or by excess mortar falling into the *flue* or by jointing material extruded from between liners and flueblocks. The *flues* should be checked to demonstrate that they have been correctly constructed and are free of restrictions and acceptably gas-tight.

A way of checking the condition of a new *flue* prior to bringing it into use would be to do the following:

a. Carry out a visual inspection of the accessible parts to check that the lining, liners or flueblocks are of the correct materials and of suitable size for the proposed application.

b. Perform checks where necessary to demonstrate that the *flue* is free from restriction: a visual check may be sufficient where the full length of the *flue* can be seen. In cases of doubt, a way of checking this would be to carry out a coring ball test or to sweep the *flue*, which may be more effective at removing flexible debris that might not be dislodged by a coring ball.

c. Check the operation and gas-tightness of the *flue* by carrying out a smoke test.

New factory-made metal chimneys

E6   A checklist for the visual inspection of a newly completed *factory-made metal chimney* is given in BS EN 15287-1:2007 and additional checks or particular variants may be included in manufacturers' *installation instructions*. Following inspection, the *chimney* should be subjected to a smoke test.

Relined flues

E7   A *flue* which has been relined may be checked to show that it is free from restrictions, such as from surplus material (where that can occur) and that it is acceptably gas-tight by using the same tests as would be applied in the case of a newly built *flue*. However, a *flue* which has been relined with a flexible metal liner in accordance with Paragraph 3.36 of this Approved Document may be assumed to be unobstructed and acceptably gas-tight. (The use of a coring ball or inappropriate sweeps brushes can seriously damage a flexible metal *flue liner*.)

Appliances

E8   Where a *combustion appliance* is provided and connected up to the flue system as part of the work, the complete system of appliance and *flue* should be tested for gas-tightness in addition to testing the *flue* separately as above. For gas appliances, an appropriate spillage test procedure is given in BS 5440-1:2008. For oil- and solid-fuel fired appliances, suitable test procedures are given in BS 5410-1:1997 and BS EN 15287-1:2007 Annex O respectively.

Flue test procedures

Coring ball test

E9   This test may be appropriate for proving the minimum diameter of circular *flues*. It may also be used to check for obstructions in square *flues* but will not detect obstructions in the corners. (A purpose-made coring ball or plate may need to be used if the *flue* is rectangular.) It is not applicable to *fluepipes* and should not be used with flexible metal *flue liners*. It should be carried out before smoke testing.

E10   A heavy ball, with a diameter about 25mm less than that of the *flue*, is lowered on a rope from the *flue outlet* to the bottom of the *flue*. If an obstruction is encountered, the blockage should be removed and the test repeated.

Smoke testing

E11   Where an existing *flue* is to be checked with a smoke test, it should first be swept.

E12   Two smoke testing procedures are described below. Test I confirms the gas-tightness of the whole *flue* and may be used for one serving a solid fuel appliance or if there is any doubt over the condition of a gas or oil *flue*. Test II may be used where the *flue* is to serve a gas-fired appliance. Neither test is a substitute for any spillage or flue draught interference test required when commissioning the appliance. Other smoke testing procedures could be used where these form part of the procedure for the installation of an approved flue or relining system

Smoke test I

E13   All doors and windows in the room served by the *flue* should be closed. The *flue* should first be warmed to establish a draught, e.g. with a blow lamp or electric heater. A suitable number of flue testing smoke pellets are placed at the base of the *flue*, such as in the *fireplace recess* or in the appliance if it is fitted, and ignited. When smoke starts to form, the base of the *flue* or fireplace opening should be sealed or the appliance should be closed, so that the smoke can only enter the *flue*. (For example, the recess opening should be closed off with a board or plate, sealed at the edges or, if the pellets are in the appliance, its doors, ashpit covers and vents should be closed.)

E14   Smoke should be seen to issue freely from the *flue outlet* or terminal. When this is established, the top of the *flue* is sealed. The full length of the *flue* should then be checked, bearing in mind Paragraph E19; there should be no significant leakage. The test should be allowed to continue for at least 5 minutes. The closures at the top and bottom of the *flue* should then be removed.

Smoke test II

E15   All doors and windows in the room served by the *flue* should be closed. The *flue* should first be warmed to establish a draught. A suitable flue-testing smoke pellet is ignited at the base of the *flue* or in the intended position of the appliance, so that the smoke is drawn into the *flue* with the rising draught. (If the pellets are placed in a recess at the base of the *flue*, the opening between the room and the recess should be partially closed, such as with a board, but so as to leave an air entry gap of about 25mm at the bottom.)

E16   Smoke should be seen to issue freely from the *flue outlet* or terminal and not to spill back into the room. There should be no significant leakage of smoke from the length of the *chimney* inside or outside of the building.

E17   Smoke tests I and II are in line with the recommendations in BS 5440-1:2008.

Notes in relation to testing

E18   Where warming of the *flue* is specified, this is intended to establish a draught, but this may take more than 10 minutes in the case of large or cold *flues*.

E19   Appliances, where fitted, should not be under fire at the time of carrying out the test. During a smoke test, smoke should not emerge from the outlet of any other *flue*, as this indicates leakage between *flues*. When checking for smoke leakage from a *flue*, it should be borne in mind that smoke from a faulty *flue* can emerge some distance away from the original fault. In such cases, the smoke could emerge from such places as barge overhangs in the end of terrace dwellings or from window reveals in cavity walls.

E20   The purpose of carrying out smoke testing is to check that flue gases will rise freely through the *flue* and to identify whether there are any faults, such as incorrectly sealed joints or damage that would cause the flue gases to escape into the dwelling.

E21   It should be noted that smoke pellets create a pressure significantly higher than the pressure required in the product standards for *natural draught chimneys* and for *flues* having a gas-tightness *designation* of N1. *Flues* to this *designation* are permitted to have a leakage rate of up to 2 litre/s/m² flue wall area. Some smoke leakage may therefore be seen during smoke tests and it can be a matter of expert judgement of whether leakage indicates failure.

E22   However, wisps of smoke visible on the outside of the *chimney* or near joints between *chimney* sections do not necessarily indicate a fault. If forceful plumes, or large volumes of smoke are seen, this could indicate a major fault such as an incorrectly made connection or joint, or a damaged section of *chimney* that requires investigation and remedial action followed by a repeat of the test.

Appendix F: Assessing air permeability of older dwellings in relation to permanent ventilation requirements

F1 The minimum requirements for permanent ventilation for certain appliances depend on a knowledge of the air-tightness of the dwelling where they are to be installed, Dwellings built after 2008 are likely to have evidence of the air-tightness either through an individual air permeability test certificate or through representative testing of the same design of dwelling on the same housing development.

F2 Older houses are unlikely to have been tested but are unlikely to achieve an air permeability of less than 5.0 $m^3/(h.m^2)$ at 50 Pa unless the building fabric has been substantially upgraded. That would include all or most of the following measures:

- Full double (or triple) glazing

- Effective closures on trickle vents and other controllable ventilation devices

- All external doors with integral draught seals and letter box seals

- Internal and external sealing around external doors and window frames

- Filled cavity or solid walls

- Impermeable overlay and edge sealing of suspended ground floors

- Careful sealing at junctions between building elements such as between walls and floors or ceilings

- Careful sealing around loft hatch

- Careful sealing around *chimney* or flue penetrations

- Careful sealing around internal soil pipe

- Careful sealing around domestic water and heating pipes passing into externally ventilated spaces

- Careful sealing of all service penetrations in the building fabric (electricity, gas, water, drainage, phone, TV aerial, etc.)

- Internal warning pipe for WC

- All cable channels for light switches and power sockets sealed

- All cable entry for lighting and ceiling roses sealed. Recessed lighting should not penetrate ceilings separating loft spaces.

F3 Failure to implement even a few of these measures will typically mean that the overall air permeability will probably exceed 5.0 $m^3/(h.m^2)$ at 50 Pa. However, individual rooms in some older houses with solid walls and solid floors can be inherently air-tight when fitted with modern glazing. The situation may therefore need to be assessed with respect both to the overall dwelling and to the individual room where the appliance is to be fitted. If in doubt then assume that the air permeability is lower than 5.0 $m^3/(h.m^2)$ at 50 Pa and fit the appropriate permanent ventilation or seek specialist advice.

Further information on sources of air leakage can be found in GPG224 *Improving airtightness in dwellings*.

Appendix G: European chimney designations

G1 This informative appendix provides a summary of the European *chimney designation* scheme. The essence of the scheme is a series of code letters based on the general *chimney designation* scheme of BS EN 1443:2003, an example of which and their explanation is given below.

Designation

G2 The *designation* of a *chimney* consists of :

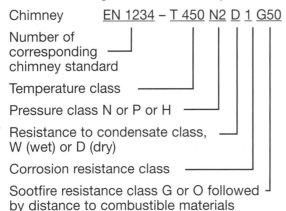

Chimney EN 1234 – T 450 N2 D 1 G50

Number of corresponding chimney standard

Temperature class

Pressure class N or P or H

Resistance to condensate class, W (wet) or D (dry)

Corrosion resistance class

Sootfire resistance class G or O followed by distance to combustible materials

G3 European *chimney* standards have been developed based on the material of the *flue liner* e.g. clay/ceramic, concrete, metal, and plastic. Some material based standards have adopted a different shortened *designation* e.g. for clay *flue liners* a *designation* Liner – EN 1457-300-A1-N2 means it is suitable for a *chimney* with the *designation* T600 N2 D 3 G, with a nominal size of 300mm.

G4 The *designation* of the corrosion resistance class of a metal *chimney* product is dealt with in BS EN 1856-1 and BS EN 1856-2 by a two-fold approach. A minimum material specification and thickness is allowed which is dependent on that which is permitted in member states regulations, where these exist. Products upon which a declaration has been made in this manner are designated Vm. The alternative approach involves the choice of one of three corrosion resistance tests. Products meeting the tests carry the *designation* V1, V2 or V3, as appropriate allow the product to be designated with the Corrosion resistance class 1, 2, or 3 respectively. The material specification still forms part of the overall *designation*, and appears alongside the 'V' letter, e.g. Vx-L40045. The material specification for the liner (or connecting pipe) is formed by the letter 'L' followed by five digits. The first two digits represent the material type and the last three digits represent the material thickness in multiples of 0.01mm.

G5 For the UK, guidance on the minimum material specification appropriate for the various applications in terms of corrosion resistance (solid fuel, gas and oil) is given in the UK National Annex to BS EN 1856-1 and -2.

For further examples of shortened *designation* refer to the specific product standards.

G6 In selecting an appliance for a given *chimney designation*, the appliance, irrespective of the fuel used, is required to generate combustion products with characteristics equal or less than those designated for the *chimney*. When selecting a *chimney* suitable for a given appliance, any *chimney* with performance characteristics equal to or higher than those appropriate for the appliance may be used.

Temperature classes

G7 Temperature classes are set out in Table G1 and
expressed as 'T' followed by a number which is less than or equal to the nominal working temperature, i.e., the average flue gas temperature obtained during the nominal/rated output test (usually the maximum operating level);

Table G1 **Temperature classes**

Temperature class	Nominal working temperature °C
T 080	≤ 80
T 100	≤ 100
T 120	≤ 120
T 140	≤ 140
T 160	≤ 160
T 200	≤ 200
T 250	≤ 250
T 300	≤ 300
T 400	≤ 400
T 450	≤ 450
T 600	≤ 600

Pressure classes

G8 Pressure classes are set out in Table G2 and expressed as either 'N', 'P' or 'H' followed by either '1' or '2'. N relates in general to *natural draught chimneys* i.e. operating under negative pressure where the value 1 or 2 allows for a different class of product; metal *chimneys* to BS EN 1856-1 have the class N1. In the UK the value N2 will be assigned as a minimum to masonry *chimneys*. P and H relate to *chimneys* which operate under positive pressure e.g. for fan assisted applications and diesel generators respectively. The pressure *designation* depends on the gas tightness it achieves, the lower number being the more onerous, the higher allowed leakage for positive pressure application being intended to external installations.

Table G2 Pressure classes

Pressure class	Test pressure Pa	Gas tightness – Maximum leakage rate $L/s/m^2$
N1	40	2.0
N2	20	3.0
P1	200	0.006
P2	200	0.120
H1	5000	0.006
H2	5000	0.120

Condensate resistance classes

G9 Condensate resistance class – expressed as either 'W' for wet or 'D' for dry operations. A product designated 'W', able to contain condensates within the *flue*, is aimed at condensing appliances. A product designated 'D' would usually have flue gas temperatures high enough to avoid condensate formation.

Corrosion resistance classes

G10 Corrosion resistance classes are set out in Table G3 – this is fuel dependant and expressed as 1, 2 or 3.

Sootfire resistance classes

G11 Sootfire resistance class – expressed as either 'G' with sootfire resistance, or 'O' without, A product assigned the *designation* 'G' has been tested at 1000°C for 30 minutes.

Distance to combustible material

G12 The *designation* of the minimum distance from the outer surface of the *chimney* to combustible material is given as xx expressed in millimetres (e.g. the distance 'x-x' identified in paragraph 1.45 and diagram 13).

Table G3 Corrosion resistance classes (from BS EN 1443-2003)

Corrosion resistance class	1 Possible fuel types	2 Possible fuel types	3 Possible fuel types
gas	Gas: sulphur-content ≤ 50 mg/m³ Natural gas L + H	Gas Natural gas L + H	Gas Natural gas L + H
liquid	Kerosene: sulphur-content ≤ 50 mg/m³	Oil: sulphur-content ≤ 0.2 mass % kerosene: sulphur-content ≥ 50 mg/m³	Oil: sulphur-content > 0.2 mass % kerosene: sulphur-content ≥ 50 mg/m³
wood		Wood in open fire places	Wood in open fire places Wood in closed stoves
coal			Coal
peat			Peat

Appendix H: Addresses

ACE (Amalgamated Chimney Engineers): White Acre, Metheringham Fen, Lincoln LN4 3AL

Tel 01526 32 30 09   Fax 01526 32 31 81

BFCMA (British Flue and Chimney Manufacturers Association): 2 Waltham Court, Milley Lane, Hare Hatch, Reading, Berkshire RG10 9TH

Tel 0118 940 3416   Fax 0118 940 6258
info@feta.co.uk   www.feta.co.uk

BRE (Building Research Establishment Ltd.): Bucknalls Lane, Garston, Watford, Hertfordshire WD25 9XX

Tel 01923 66 4000   Fax 01923 66 4010
enquiries@bre.co.uk   www.bre.co.uk

BSI (British Standards Institution): 389 Chiswick High Road, London W4 4AL

Tel 020 8996 9000   Fax 020 8996 7400
www.bsigroup.com

CIBSE (Chartered Institution of Building Services Engineers): 222 Balham High Road, London SW12 9BS

Tel 020 8675 5211   Fax 020 8675 5449
www.cibse.org

Gas Safe Register: PO Box 6804, Basingstoke RG24 4NB

Tel 0800 408 5500
www.gassaferegister.co.uk

Environment Agency: Rio House, Waterside Drive, Aztec West, Almondsbury, Bristol BS32 4UD

08708 506506
www.environment-agency.gov.uk

Environment Agency Emergency Hotline
0800 80 70 60

HETAS (Heating Equipment Testing and Approval Scheme): Orchard Business Centre, Stoke Orchard, Cheltenham, Gloucestershire GL52 7RZ

Tel 0845 634 5626
www.hetas.co.uk

HSE (Health and Safety Executive): (1G) Redgrave Court, Merton Road, Merseyside L20 7HS

Tel 0845 345 0055
www.hse.gov.uk

HSE Infoline: 0845 345 0055

Gas safety advice line: 0800 300 363

IGEM (Institution of Gas Engineers & Managers): IGEM House, High Street, Kegworth, Derbyshire DE74 2DA

Tel 0844 375 4436   Fax 01509 678198
www.igem.org.uk

UKLPG: Unit 14, Bow Court, Fletchworth Gate Burnsall Road, Coventry CV5 6SP

www.uklpg.org

NACE (National Association of Chimney Engineers): PO Box 849, Metheringham Lincoln LN4 3WU

Tel 01526 322555
www.nace.org.uk

NACS (National Association of Chimney Sweeps): Unit 15, Emerald Way, Stone Business Park, Stone, Staffordshire ST15 0SR

Tel 01785 811732   Fax 01785 811712
nacs@chimneyworks.co.uk
www.chimneyworks.co.uk

NFA (National Fireplace Association): PO Box 583, High Wycombe, Bucks HP15 6XT

Tel 0845 643 1901   Fax 0845 643 1902
www.fireplace.co.uk

OFTEC (Oil Firing Technical Association Ltd): Foxwood House, Dobbs Lane, Kesgrave Ipswich IP5 2QQ

Tel 0845 65 85 080   Fax 0845 65 85 181
enquiries@oftec.org   www.oftec.org

SFA (Solid Fuel Association): 7 Swanwick Court, Alfreton, Derbyshire DE55 7AS

Tel 01773 835 400   Fax 01773 834 351
sfa@solidfuel.co.uk www.solidfuel.co.uk

Standards referred to

BS 41:1973 (1998)
Specification for cast iron spigot and socket flue or smoke pipes and fittings.

BS EN 303-1:1999
Heating Boilers. Heating boilers with forced draught burners. Terminology general requirements, testing and marking.

BS 476-4:1970 (2007)
Fire tests on building materials and structures. Non-combustibility test for materials. AMD 2483 and AMD 4390.

BS 476-11:1982 (2007)
Fire tests on building materials and structures. Method for assessing the heat emission from building materials.

BS 476-20:1987
Fire tests on building materials and structures. Method for determination of the fire resistance of elements of construction (general principles).

BS 476-21:1987
Fire tests on building materials and structures. Methods for determination of the fire resistance of loadbearing elements of construction.

BS 476-22:1987
Fire tests on building materials and structures. Methods for determination of the fire resistance of non-loadbearing elements of construction.

BS EN 449:2002 + a1:2007
Specification for Dedicated Liquid Petroleum Gas Appliances. Domestic Flueless Space Heaters (including Diffusive Catalytic Combustion Heaters).

BS 715:2005
Specification for metal flue pipes, fittings, terminals and accessories for gas-fired appliances with a rated input not exceeding 60kW. AMD 8413.

BS 799-5:1987
Oil Burning Equipment. Specification for Oil Storage Tanks.

BS 1181:1999
Specification for clay flue linings and flue terminals.

BS 1251:1987
Specification for open fireplace components.

BS EN 1443:2003
Chimneys. General Requirements.

BS 1449-2:1983
Specification for stainless and heat-resisting steel plate, sheet and strip. AMD 4807, AMD 6646 and AMD 8832.

BS EN 10268:2006
Cold rolled steel flat products with high yield strength for cold forming. Technical delivery conditions.

BS EN 1457:2009
Chimneys. Clay/ceramic flue liners. Requirements and test methods.

BS EN 1806:2006
Chimneys. Clay/ceramic flue blocks for single wall chimneys. Requirements and test methods.

BS 1846-1:1994
Glossary of Terms Relating to Solid Fuel Burning Equipment. 1994 Domestic appliances.

BS EN 1856-1:2003
Chimneys. Requirements for metal chimneys. System chimney products.

BS EN 1856-2:2004
Chimneys. Requirements for metal chimneys. Metal liners and connecting flue pipes.

BS EN 1857:2003 + A1:2008
Chimneys. Components. Concrete flue liners.

BS EN 1858:2003
Chimneys. Components. Concrete flue blocks.

BS EN 1859:2009
Chimneys. Metal chimneys. Test methods.

BS 2869:2006
Fuel oils for agricultural, domestic and industrial engines and boilers. Specification.

BS EN 1859:2000
Chimney, Metal chimneys. Test methods.

BS 2869-2:1998
Fuel oils for non-Marine use. Specification for fuel oil for agricultural and industrial engines and burners (Classes A2, C1, C2, D, E, F, G and H). AMD 6505.

BS 4543-1:1990
Factory-made insulated chimneys. Methods of test. AMD 8379.

BS 4543-2:1990
Factory-made insulated chimneys. Specification for chimneys with stainless steel flue linings for use with solid fuel fired appliances. AMD 8380.

BS 4543-3:1990
Factory-made insulated chimneys. Specification for chimneys with stainless steel fluelining for use with oil fired appliances. AMD 8381.

BS 4876:1984
Specification for performance requirements for domestic flued oil burning appliances (including test procedures).

BS 5410-1:1997
Code of practice for oil firing. Installations up to 44kW output capacity for space heating and hot water supply purposes. AMD 3637.

BS 5410-2:1978
Code of practice for oil firing. Installations of 45 kW and above output capacity for space heating, hot water and steam supply services.

BS 5440-1:2008
Installation and maintenance of flues and ventilation for gas appliances of rated input not exceeding 70kW net (1st, 2nd and 3rd family gases). Specification for Installation and maintenance of flues.

BS 5440-2:2000
Installation and maintenance of flues and ventilation for gas appliances of rated input not exceeding 70kW net (1st, 2nd and 3rd Family Gases). Specification for installation and maintenance of ventilation for gas appliances.

BS 5482-1:2005
Code of practice for domestic butane- and propane-gas-burning installations. Installations at permanent dwellings, residential park homes and commercial premises, with installation pipework sizes not exceeding DN 25 for steel and DN 28 for corrugated stainless steel or copper.

BS 5546:2000
Specification for installation of hot water supplies for domestic purposes, using gas fired appliances of rated input not exceeding 70kW.

BS 5854:1980 (1996)
Code of practice for flues and flue structures in buildings.

BS 5864:2004
Specification for Installation in Domestic Premises of Gas-Fired Ducted-Air Heaters of Rated Input Not Exceeding 60kW.

BS 5871-1:2005
Specification for Installation of Gas Fires, Convector Heaters, Fire/Back Boilers and Decorative Fuel Effect Gas Appliances. Gas Fires, Convector Heaters and Fire/Back Boilers and heating stoves (1st, 2nd and 3rd Family Gases).

BS 5871-2:2005

Specification for Installation of Gas Fires, Convector Heaters, Fire/Back Boilers and Decorative Fuel Effect Gas Appliances. Inset Live Fuel Effect Gas Fires of Heat Input Not Exceeding 15kW (2nd and 3rd Family Gases).

BS 5871-3:2005
Specification for Installation of Gas Fires, Convector Heaters, Fire/Back Boilers and Decorative Fuel Effect Gas Appliances. Decorative Fuel Effect Gas Appliances of Heat Input Not Exceeding 20kW (2nd and 3rd Family Gases).

BS 6172:2004
Specification for Installation of Domestic Gas Cooking Appliances (1st, 2nd and 3rd Family Gases).

BS 6173:2001
Specification for Installation of Gas Fired Catering Appliances for Use in All Types of Catering Establishments (1st, 2nd and 3rd Family Gases).

BS EN 15287-1:2007
Chimneys. Design, installation and commissioning of chimneys. Chimneys for non-roomsealed heating appliances.

BS 6798:2009
Specification for Installation of Gas-Fired Boilers of Rated Input Not Exceeding 70kW.

BS 6999:1989 (1996)
Specification for Vitreous-Enamelled Low-Carbon-Steel Fluepipes, Other Components and Accessories for Solid-Fuel-Burning Appliances with a Maximum Rated Output of 45kW.

BS 7435-1:1991 (1998)
Fibre Cement Flue Pipes, Fittings and Terminals. Specification for Light Quality Fibre Cement Flue pipes, Fittings and Terminals.

BS 7435-2:1991
Fibre Cement Flue Pipes, Fittings and Terminals. Specifications for heavy quality cement flue pipes, fittings and terminals.

BS 7566:
Installation of Factory-Made Chimneys to BS 4543 for Domestic Appliances

BS 7566-1:1992 (1998)
Installation of Factory-Made Chimneys to BS 4543 for Domestic Appliances. Method of Specifying Installation Design Information.

BS 7566-2:1992 (1998)
Installation of Factory-Made Chimneys to BS 4543 for Domestic Appliances. Specification for Installation Design.

BS 7566-4:1992 (1998)
Installation of Factory-Made Chimneys to BS 4543 for Domestic Appliances. Recommendations for Installation Design and Installation.

BS 8303-1:1994
Installation of Domestic Heating and Cooking Appliances Burning Solid Mineral Fuels, Specification for the Design of Installations.

BS 8303-2:1994
Installation of Domestic Heating and Cooking Appliances Burning Solid Mineral Fuels, Specification for Installing and Commissioning on Site.

BS 8303-3:1994
Installation of Domestic Heating and Cooking Appliances Burning Solid Mineral Fuels, Recommendations for Design and on Site Installation.

BS EN 10088-1:2005
Stainless Steels. List of Stainless Steels.

BS EN 13384-1:2002 + A2:2008
Chimneys. Thermal and fluid dynamic calculation methods. Chimneys serving one appliance.

BS EN 14213:2003
Heating fuels. Fatty acid methyl esters (FAME). Requirements and test methods.

BS EN 15287-1:2007
Chimneys. Design, installation and commissioning of chimneys.

Other publications referred to

Government

Approved Document J: 2002 Edition: Supplementary Guidance on the UK Implementation of European Standards for Chimneys and Flues, ODPM (2004). *Available to download from www.planningportal.gov.uk.*

The Gas Safety (Installations and Use) Regulations 1998.

Gas Appliances (Safety) Regulations 1995.

Workplace, Safety and Welfare, Workplace (Health, Safety and Welfare) Regulations 1992, Approved Code of Practice L24, HSE Books (1992). ISBN 978 0 71760 413 5

Guide to Condensing Boiler Installation Assessment Procedure for Dwellings. Office of the Deputy Prime Minister (2005). ISBN 978 1 85112 784 9

Building Research Establishment

BR 414 (2001) Protective measures for housing on gas contaminated land. ISBN 978 1 86081 460 0

BR 211 (2007) Radon: guidance on protective measures for new buildings (including supplementary advice for extensions, conversions and refurbishment) (2007 edition).

Chartered Institution of Building Services Engineers

CIBSE Guide B: Heating, Ventilating, Air Conditioning and Refrigeration, (2005). ISBN 978 1 90328 758 3

Energy Saving Trust

GPG224 Improving airtightness in dwellings (2005).

Environment Agency

The Control of Pollution (Oil Storage) (England) Regulations (2001).

Pollution Prevention Guidelines PPG2 – Above Ground Oil Storage Tanks (2004).

Pollution Prevention Guidelines PPG27- Installation, Decommissioning and Removal of Underground Storage Tanks (2002).

Masonry Bunds for Oils Storage Tanks, CIRIA/ Environment Agency Joint Guidelines

Concrete Bunds for Oils Storage Tanks, CIRIA/ Environment Agency Joint Guidelines

Available to download from http://publications. environment-agency.gov.uk.

Health and Safety Executive

Safety in the installation and use of gas systems and appliances, Approved Code of Practice and Guidance L56, HSE Books. ISBN 978 0 71761 635 0

HETAS

HETAS Information Paper 1/007 Chimneys in Thatched Properties (2009).

Oil Firing Technical Association (OFTEC)

OFTEC Oil Fired Appliance Standard. OFS A100. Heating Boilers with Atomising Burners. Outputs up to 70kW. Maximum Operating Pressures of 3 Bar (2004).

OFTEC Oil Fired Appliance Standard. OFS A101. Oil Fired Cookers with Atomising or Vaporising Burners with or without Boilers. Heat Outputs up to 45kW (2004).

OFTEC Technical Book 3: Installation requirements for oil fired equipment 1st Edition (2006).

OFS T100 Oil Firing Equipment Standard – Polyethylene Oil Storage Tanks for Distillate Fuels (2008).

OFS T200 Oil Firing Equipment Standard – Steel Oil Storage Tanks and Tank Bunds for use with Distillate Fuels, Lubrication Oils and Waste Oils (2007).

UKLPG

Code of Practice 1 Bulk LPG Storage at Fixed Installations Part1: Design, Installation and Operation of Vessels Located Above Ground (January 2009).

Index